W9-CHS-694

Make-Believe

Games & Activities for IMAGINATIVE PLAY

A Book for Parents, Teachers, and the Young Children in Their Lives

To our granddaughters
Cory, Grace, Laurel, Olivia, and Chloe

Make-Believe

Games & Activities for

IMAGINATIVE

PLAY

A Book for Parents, Teachers, and the Young Children in Their Lives

by Dorothy G. Singer, Ed.D.,

and Jerome L. Singer, Ph.D.

MAGINATION PRESS • WASHINGTON, DC

Copyright © 2001 by Magination Press. All rights reserved.
Except as permitted under the United States Copyright Act of 1976, no part of this publication
may be reproduced or distributed in any form or by any means, or stored in a database or
retrieval system, without the prior written permission of the publisher.

Published by
MAGINATION   PRESS
An Educational Publishing Foundation Book
American Psychological Association
750 First Street, NE
Washington, DC 20002

For more information about our books, including a complete catalog, please write to us,
call 1-800-374-2721, or visit our website at www.maginationpress.com

Library of Congress Cataloging-in-Publication Data

Singer, Dorothy G.
Make-believe : games and activities for imaginative play : a book for parents, teachers,
and the young children in their lives / by Dorothy G. Singer and Jerome L. Singer.
p.   cm.
Includes bibliographical references.
ISBN 1-55798-717-3
1. Play. 2. Educational games. 3. Creative activities and seat work.
I. Singer, Jerome L. II. Title.

LB1137 .S559 2000
372.13—dc21

00-028444

Manufactured in the United States of America
10 9 8 7 6 5 4 3 2 1

TABLE OF CONTENTS

PREFACE

The human imagination is one of the great untapped resources in the growing child's ability to learn, to evolve a sense of self, and to simply enjoy the pleasures of his or her own creative capacities. Almost all preschool children naturally develop and expand their imaginative skills. However, with additional encouragement and direction from parents and early teachers, the scope of young children's imaginative play can broaden considerably, with rewarding results.

Currently there is a concern in our society about the loss of innocence and the disappearance of childhood, notably with regard to the widespread availability to children of sexual and violent images through television and movies. At the same time, we are seeing a trend toward training babies and preschoolers to appreciate art and music, to grasp mathematical concepts, and to learn to recognize words—sometimes before they can walk! Thus, as society laments a loss of innocence, it is also moving toward an acceleration of particular skills, including computer literacy, that we believe should come about mainly through a child's natural development and inherent curiosity.

What is a parent's or teacher's role in implementing a fully realized childhood? Educators are concerned about the shortage of science and math teachers, but one hears little about the need to enhance imagination and fantasy. It seems that the pendulum is swinging back to the days of the *Sputnik* crisis, when the United States found it was losing the space race with the Soviet Union. In the desire to be first among nations, and perhaps even among neighbors, Americans are deemphasizing the need for children to be children. Our society is disinclined to allow them to explore their world at their own pace with the appropriate tools for such exploration, and with the adult sanction that it is good to play. With this book, we are urging parents, teachers, all caregivers of young children, and students in courses in education and child development to turn their attention to what the early 20th-century Dutch psychologist Karl Groos called "the task of childhood": play.

Our own 30 years of research on children's imaginative play suggest not only that such play is entertaining for children, but also that it prepares them for many useful school readiness and life skills. These skills are outlined in the "Skills Developed in Make-Believe" chart on pages 16-19, and are discussed in detail in chapter 1, "What Make-Believe Can Do for Children."

Make Believe: Games and Activities for Imaginative Play has grown out of extensive research by ourselves and others in direct involvement with preschoolers. We have explored a range of exercises and games designed to help preschool children expand their imaginative horizons and enjoy their own play more. The procedures, suggestions, exercises, and games presented in this book will help parents and teachers, and any other adults who interact with young children, play more effectively with children. They are also geared toward fostering the independent development of children's imaginative resources.

Our format consists of brief general discussions of the importance of different aspects of make-believe play and imagination in healthy growth, followed by a series of specific exercises or games suitable for use at home or in the daycare center, nursery school, or kindergarten. We have tested these activities with a wide variety of children from ages two through five; the games have been used by other adults as well. They are based on the best scientific evidence available, are simple and practical, and are also such fun that parents and teachers will find the time they spend with young children much more enjoyable.

For parents and teachers interested in books and music that can heighten the child's imagination, we include an extensive list of materials appropriate for preschool-age children. In addition, at the back of this volume is a reference list for readers who would like to explore the psychological research literature on make-believe and sociodramatic play. The main thesis of this book, however, is that fantasy and creativity can be stimulated with a minimum of props. The enthusiasm of a concerned and knowledgeable adult, who uses some of the games, stories, and exercises we describe, is the best tool for arousing the child's imaginative resources.

Dorothy G. Singer, Ed.D.
Jerome L. Singer, Ph.D.
YALE UNIVERSITY

INTRODUCTION

Both parents and teachers will find that the games in this book can help children learn how to expand their imaginations. Children with a repertoire of make-believe play skills are more self-reliant and demand less of your time as they follow their own creative direction with a game, embellishing it with details and making up new variations. The general benefits of imaginative play are discussed in chapter 1, "What Make-Believe Can Do for Children," and the specific benefits of focused activity areas, such as motor, sensory, and role-playing, are presented at the beginning of each activity chapter.

The child's environment at home or in preschool is undoubtedly encouraging growth in these skills already, since those parents and teachers who are reading this book are likely to be tuned in quite well to their children's needs already. The activities in this book should therefore be viewed as extras. They are meant to be the tools that you can choose to use or not when you're feeling like spending a pleasurable time with your children. Most of all, we want you and your children to have fun while they just happen to be learning.

For Parents

Susan and Peter are both employed full-time outside the home. Mornings are like a fast-paced television program. Each parent is rushing around to see that the children are dressed and fed, and have their lunches and backpacks ready to go. They're getting dressed themselves, going over the day's schedule with each other, and praying that no one has a cold, because that would mean scrambling to find a sitter or deciding which parent will take the day off. Evenings are about the same, except Susan's and Peter's energy levels are lower, and weekends are when the family catches up on all the chores that have been neglected during the week. In the midst of their fast-paced lives, Susan and Peter are concerned about their children. The phrase "quality time" torments them, and often they wonder if they are offering their preschoolers the kind of activities and interactions that children need in order to develop into truly well-rounded people.

The concerns of families that are structured differently—one parent in an office and the other at home, for example, or one or both parents employed or attending school part-time—are much the same. American parents tend to lead busy lives. Most wonder if they are making enough time for their families, and if the children are getting the right kind of attention and involvement from mom and dad.

Many parents wonder if their children are overscheduled in lessons and organized activities, others worry that they let their children watch too much television, and some are concerned that even though their children enjoy playing with computers or video games they are missing out on social interaction with real people.

The make-believe games in this book offer parents a *humanizing* approach to engaging their children in fun activities centered around play, imagination, and interaction. A number of the games are very simple and can easily be carried out within five or ten minutes. Others can be incorporated into chores, errands, and daily routines such as meals and bath time to make these necessary activities more pleasurable and transform them into shared moments. Many will seem familiar and may be variations on games you have already played with your child. The activities may even help you begin to remember your own joyful childhood experiences. These memories may in turn serve as the impetus for you to engage in more make-believe play with your children.

Approach this book like a cookbook or other reference tool, and start with the games that appeal the most or those that you're most comfortable trying. Perhaps chapter 10, "Using Television for Imaginative Growth" is the place to begin, since you probably watch some television programs with your child. Move on to other games at your own pace. The chart on pages 16-19 indicates the aspects of child development that the activities enhance. Remember that children progress at their own, individual rate. A game that one three-year-old may love can be too easy and boring, or too difficult and frustrating, for another. Most of the games can be modified to suit all children between ages two to five. Try the easier ones first, and the more challenging ones the next time. Experiment, embellish, and enjoy! It's important that both you and your child experience success and fun.

For Teachers

Cathy is a teacher at a daycare center. The enrollment of children in the center has increased over the years, but Cathy's director still must comply with state regulations and make sure that there are enough teachers for each class. The pool of volunteer parents has shrunk over the years as more mothers have become employed and the number of single parents has grown. Cathy finds that she has little time to spend with small groups of children, but when she does have the time, she recognizes the need for imaginative play.

Cathy has read a good deal about the importance of readying children for kindergarten, but she does not want to teach cognitive skills such as numbers, colors, shapes, and the alphabet in a dry and rote fashion. She wonders if children can learn these concepts through imaginative play. Cathy also believes that it is important for children to learn how to express themselves clearly. And she is interested in teaching her children to share, take turns, and cooperate—the social skills that are useful if not essential both in preschool and as the children prepare to enter kindergarten. Teachers such as Cathy will find that the games in this book address many of their concerns. The make-believe activities described here help children in the development of all these skills, and more.

As a teacher, you may want to play these games when you have extra help in the classroom, when either a teacher assistant or a volunteer is there to lend a hand. Trying to play with a few children at a time may be difficult when there is a class of 20 preschoolers to keep busy. Instead, choose a different group of children each day during free play, and give them your attention by starting them on a game and checking occasionally to see how the story is going. If the children get bogged down, simply introduce the next element to keep the game going. Other games are well-suited to large groups. Restaurant and camping games easily involve large numbers of children, as do activities involving motor skills or demonstrating emotions.

The chart on pages 16-19 can be an effective tool for teachers. If a particular child in the class needs special attention, the chart can help you find the appropriate exercises. It is also useful for suggesting specific areas of development that teachers may wish to work on with the entire class. Together, the chart and the activities can help you foster the skills that will give your children the best possible start in the school years that lie ahead, and at the same time allow them to do now what they do best: play.

SKILLS DEVELOPED IN MAKE-BELIEVE

AREAS FOR GROWTH AND SKILL DEVELOPMENT

RELATED GAMES AND ACTIVITIES

Emotions

1. Learn how to recognize, understand, interpret, and convey feelings using the face, parts of the body, and the whole body.

2. Feel worthwhile, gain self-confidence, and develop a sense of trust in relationships with others.

CHAPTER 3
"Make-Believe Feet" (page 60) demonstrates the way we walk to show emotions.

CHAPTER 5
The activity group "Emotional Awareness and Sensitivity" (pages 79-81) presents several emotion-awareness games. In particular, "Making Faces" (page 79) explores emotions reflected in facial expressions.

CHAPTER 6
All activities explore and develop emotional awareness. The "Poems" (pages 92-93) and "Songs" (pages 94-95) groups help children articulate and express feelings. The "Stories" group (pages 96-97) helps children convey emotions and provides opportunities to foster empathy. "Puppet Show" (page 97) helps shy children express feelings.

CHAPTER 7
All activities in this chapter that deals with social role-playing help a child understand the relationships to people in various roles, including teacher, doctor, waiter, and so on (pages 102-109). Feelings can be expressed in this make-believe play. Self-healing can take place. Emotional growth is fostered.

CHAPTER 10
Discussion of television programs and acting out the stories seen on television help develop emotional awareness (pages 152-165).

| AREAS FOR GROWTH AND SKILL DEVELOPMENT | RELATED GAMES AND ACTIVITIES |

Creativity

1. Nourish the natural predisposition for exploration and curiosity, arousing interest and maintaining a sense of wonder.

2. Develop outlets for creative expression, including music, storytelling, poetry, and role-playing.

CHAPTER 4

All activities in this chapter, designed to heighten sensory awareness, help a child develop curiosity (pages 66-75). "Hearing" (pages 71-73) and "Seeing" (pages 73-75) games, in particular, provide opportunities for creative expression.

CHAPTER 5

"Let's Be Animals" (page 80) and "Basket of Hats" (page 81) encourage creative expression through role-playing animals and people. "Magician" (page 83) affords children a broad opportunity to fashion objects out of clay and change them. "Four Seasons" (pages 84-85) enables children to envision and enact possible things to do during each season of the year. "Airplanes in Flight" (pages 86-87) allows children to invent places and imagine the inhabitants and environments.

CHAPTER 6

The entire chapter focuses on creative expression through poems, music, and stories (pages 98-115).

CHAPTER 7

This chapter on social role-playing is devoted to games that use familiar play themes—doctor, post office, car wash—as starting points. Children elaborate on these themes and invent new roles, environments, and interactions (pages 98-115).

CHAPTER 9

"Songs" (page 143), "Partner Drawing" (page 144), and "Imaginary Places" (page 144) in the "Games Worth Waiting For" activity group provide opportunities for creative expression in various forms. The role-playing games in the "Outings" group (pages 144-145) encourage children to invent and enact new people and situations. "Sick in Bed" (page 148) presents a range of games that involve music, storytelling, role-playing, and sculpting objects from clay. "Birthday Parties" (pages 150-151) presents a range of creative activities for groups of young children.

CHAPTER 10

"TV Tunes" (page 166), "Commercial Break" (page 167), and "You're on TV!" (page 167) encourage original expression through interpretive dance and dramatized storytelling.

AREAS FOR GROWTH AND SKILL DEVELOPMENT	RELATED GAMES AND ACTIVITIES

Motor

1. Develop coordination in both large and fine motor tasks, and learn physical control of the body.

2. Develop confidence, and a sense of mastery and competence.

CHAPTER 3
Fine motor activities are emphasized in the "Finger Games" (pages 51-53), "Finger Make-Believe" (pages 53-54), and "Hand Games" (pages 55-56) activity groups. The "Feet and Toes" (pages 57-60) activity group includes balance games and exercises that include both fine and large motor skills. Large motor activities are emphasized in the "All of Me" group (pages 60-61).

Sensory

1. Stimulate imagery through sensory awareness.

2. Develop a richer appreciation for and perception of the environment.

CHAPTER 4
This entire chapter is devoted to sharpening the awareness and experience of all five senses (pages 62-75).

Social

1. Learn how to get along with others.

2. Learn how to behave appropriately.

3. Learn how to become interdependent members of a community.

4. Understand the roles and functions of individuals in society.

5. Acquire self-confidence.

6. Acquire the ability to adapt in new situations.

CHAPTER 5
The "Emotional Awareness and Sensitivity" activity group (pages 79-81) helps children learn to recognize, identify, and express emotions and develop empathy.

CHAPTER 7
This chapter concentrates on developing skill with social roles and relationships through role-playing (pages 98-115).

CHAPTER 10
This chapter on constructive uses of television discusses the effect of TV on social skills in "The Bad News" and "The Good News" (pages 154-158). Suggestions for helping children develop social awareness are made in "Watching Television With Your Child" (pages 164-165). The activity "Getting Along" (pages 166-167) focuses on a range of interpersonal skills.

AREAS FOR GROWTH AND SKILL DEVELOPMENT	RELATED GAMES AND ACTIVITIES

Cognitive

1. Expand vocabulary, and encourage descriptive and colorful word choices.

2. Learn numbers and basic mathematical concepts.

3. Acquire and understand concepts of time, space, distance, size, and direction.

4. Learn about nature and natural phenomena.

5. Understand logical sequences.

CHAPTER 1

As noted in "Verbal Skills" (page 25), all make-believe games contribute to language acquisition. Any of the games described in this book, especially the more complex games involving role-playing, will enhance vocabulary.

CHAPTER 3

"Finger Counting" (page 51), "Finger Naming" (page 52), "Colored Rings" (page 52), and "Right Hand, Left Hand" (page 56) focus on numbers, colors, direction, and identification.

CHAPTER 4

The activities in this chapter focus on physical and natural phenomena and processes as experienced through the five sense (pages 62-75).

CHAPTER 5

In the "Transformations" activity group (pages 82-83), children learn the concepts of size and change. The "Developing Sequence" group (pages 84-87) teaches children that events generally occur in a logical and predictable order.

CHAPTER 10

The effective use of educational television programs is described throughout this chapter, particularly in "Choosing the Right Program" and "Watching Television With Your Child" (pages 159-165). The game "Let's Find It" (page 166) focuses on identifying patterns, numbers, colors, and other cognitive concepts. "Weather Watch" (page 166) develops awareness and understanding of weather features and patterns.

CHAPTER ONE

What Make-Believe Can Do For Children

Four-year-old Jenny and Carlos are busy at play in a nursery school. They are climbing on the indoor jungle gym, trying to get across as fast as they possibly can, then demonstrating their strength by swinging higher and higher before jumping down to the ground. Perhaps Jenny and Carlos are pretending they are sea adventurers of old, climbing into an ancient fortress to rescue an imprisoned member of their band.

Paul and Erica are piling one block on top of another to see how high a tower they can build before it falls. They make believe the towers are skyscrapers being shaken by earthquakes. After a few of these pretend natural disasters, they become young architects and engineers, organizing their blocks into "cities" and "space stations."

Olivia and Ben are seated in the corner sandbox. They are

pretending it contains an island, to which a little pipe cleaner boat floating on make-believe water is traveling back and forth. Amid much "splashing," Ben shouts, "Hurricane! Danger!" and tries to move the boat safely away from the flying sand.

All of these children are using whatever they have at hand—swings, blocks, sand—to represent objects or situations quite different from what they actually are. Making believe and pretending are among the many wonders of the experience of being human. In comparison, young animals engage in various types of play, carrying out a good deal of rough-and-tumble. Chimpanzees and fairly advanced monkeys even appear to pretend to threaten and mollify each other. In particular, chimpanzees make a kind of "play face" as if to indicate that their pushing and shoving are not to be taken as attacks, and by this means they avoid getting into dangerous fights. However, animal pretend play has none of the complexities of caretaking, make-believe teaching and doctoring, and high adventure of exploration, crisis, and conflict that are standard fare in the play of human four- and five-year-olds.

The play of animals is very much like what they spend the rest of their time doing: grooming, fighting for territory, feeding. Their play could never be categorized as imaginative. The play of human children, like other creatures, may mimic some actions of adults. However, it also includes a vast array of potential and even impossible behaviors that from this early age hint at the limitless range of the human imagination.

THE IMPORTANCE OF MAKE-BELIEVE

Ben and Olivia can certainly tell the difference between a pipe cleaner and a boat. What they are doing is using whatever implements are available, some more realistic in appearance than others, and filling in other details with the use of imagery—the ability to form mental images with the imagination. As they play, they constantly change the time and space relationships in situations, and project images into the future. Of course, a four-year-old may not stick with the story line very long. He may get some of the details mixed up, or terminate the game abruptly and move on to another activity.

The thought process of the child who uses blocks to build a space station is not all that different from that of the film director working with a script. From bare words on a page, the director envisions an elaborate complex of physical settings and human interactions, which he or she will actually translate through the camera into a form that others can share. Similarly, the child begins with blocks and twigs and spoons, and drawing on the memories she has been storing since infancy, she too tries to develop a setting, a series of characters, and a rudimentary plot.

By 18 months of age, children already show signs of make-believe in their play, "feeding" themselves with empty spoons or

> **"THE ABILITY TO MAKE BELIEVE IS BASIC TO A WELL-ROUNDED, FULFILLED HUMAN BEING."**

cups and exclaiming "Yummy!" The child's tendency to play and replay past events or to anticipate future ones through imagery seems to be a basic capacity of the brain that can be sustained and enlarged by the encouragement of adults.

Our human capacity to plan ahead, whether for moments, days, or years, is built to a certain extent around our playful daydreams of possible events in the future and our role in them. The great German neurologist Dr. Kurt Goldstein proposed that the highest human function is our ability "to take an attitude toward the possible." In many different ways we use our ability for make-believe or fantasy as a means of anticipating practical consequences.

We may play out in our mind's eye certain financial transactions we hope to undertake. We may picture how we ought to behave in certain social situations that are upcoming. Sometimes we try to experience the emotions of an important person in our lives by picturing that individual in different situations. We attempt to feel in ourselves what he or she may be feeling. This is empathy, a critical feature of love and intimacy, and of mature concern for others.

A childhood rich in fantasy play thus lays the foundation for an adult life that is rich with not only imagination and a sense of playfulness but also with adaptive skills that are useful and necessary for dealing with a complex society. Pretending and make-believe, activities that start early in childhood and continue into adult life, are basic to a rounded, fulfilled human being.

SPECIFIC BENEFITS OF MAKE–BELIEVE FOR CHILDREN

Imaginative play can make for a generally happy childhood, a benefit that is worthwhile in itself. Make-believe games also carry very specific advantages for the child that have been documented by scientific research.

Better Mood

Studies indicate that children who engage in make-believe games of various kinds are more likely to be smiling and to be giving other signs of elation, happiness, and contentment. Children with less capacity for spontaneous make-believe are more likely to appear either sluggish or sad, or to become aggressive. They disrupt the play of others, find themselves the object of their parents' or teachers' anger, and are often labeled "bad" at an early age.

Self-Awareness

Children who pretend to feed themselves with an empty cup, or to feed their mommy or a toy "horsey," are making important strides in self-development. They are identifying unreality but using it playfully; they are transforming empty to full, and the toy animal to a real one or to a human baby. Most of all, they are developing a sense of self and demonstrating their control over everyday objects. This sense of power over their movements and their bodies, as well as over the environment, emerges from manipulating small objects and pretending with them.

Imagery Skill

One of the great human resources for organizing and using complex information is imagery, our ability to mentally replay a sensation that has already passed us by in time. We can recreate a smell or taste or sound or sight that is no longer present by using the great storehouse of memories that are essential to learning and intellectual growth. Children's make-believe games depend heavily on the capacity for imagery. Watch, for example, as a child pretends that a piece of fabric, a slipper, or a small bag of rice is a baby who moves or talks or wets or smells. The more practice children get with imagery, the more refined their imagery skills become. Later, imagery adds a kind of richness or savor to the adult's life by sharpening the senses; through imagery we can recapture the smells of favorite foods, the beauty of a particular sunset, or the melody of a favorite song.

Verbal Skills

Young children do not appear to "think to themselves" nearly as much as adults. Much of what is viewed as thought or the stream of consciousness is expressed outwardly by preschool children in words, phrases, movements, and sound effects. In pretending, therefore, the child blurts out everything he is experiencing or knows.

Also, with his words, sounds, phrases, and shouts, he often changes his voice to represent different characters and—to the amusement of any grown-ups nearby—imitates adult expressions. By hearing their own words and those of their playmates, children are in effect practicing vocabulary, learning new ways to express themselves, and picking up phrases or nuances of the language. If a child needs a word for a person in space ("astronaut") or for a boat that goes under the ocean ("submarine"), he can ask an adult or a playmate. As he repeats the word aloud and uses it in a play context, he is enriching his vocabulary.

Emotional Awareness and Sensitivity

During make-believe play, a child may take the part of several characters, or change from her own role as a child to that of a parent or doctor or teacher. In doing this, she will not only mimic the phrases of the adult but also will be trying on the emotions and sense of concern that adults show for children. Such play then becomes the basis for developing feelings of sympathy and empathy, and also helps the child later in grasping the more subtle aspects of an adult's communication.

Learning Roles for New Social Situations

By shifting from "I'm the daddy" to "I'm the baby" or "I'm the teacher" or "I'm the police officer," children develop an awareness of the different figures they see about them and what their functions may be. As a result, they can be more comfortable in new situations. For example, the child who plays "school" can find that real school seems less frightening or strange. Studies of children in Israel who were unfamiliar with the routines or demands of school showed that when some of the children were provided with opportunities to play make-believe school games, they adjusted to school more easily later on than the children who did not play such games. Even in games that are less closely related to real possibilities, such as adventure or exploration games, make-believe play helps the child absorb material found in history lessons, news broadcasts, and so on.

Flexibility in New Social Situations

Children often behave in ways that are impulsive, self-centered, or inflexible in the face of new situations. Such behavior occurs because youngsters haven't had enough experience to make sense of the new setting. Young children also lack time perspective—the ability (based on experience) to realize that certain events have a natural sequence and that the desired outcome will eventually emerge. They become impulsive if they have to wait for a hamburger to cook, for their turn on the swings, for a haircut, for their appointment with the doctor. Pretending, talking to themselves, and imaginative play help children develop self-control during such waiting situations and make them less likely to become upset or aggressive.

Moreover, make-believe can transform an otherwise dull or tedious situation into a positive experience. Consider the youngster marking time in a drab airport lounge. With a small box and the miniature figures in his pocket, the child skilled in make-believe can create an exciting adventure of travel to far-off lands or planets, complete with monsters, strange natives, or physical dangers.

While he remains absorbed in the game, time passes quickly, the flight arrives, and before he knows it here comes Grandma through the gate. But the child without the resources of make-believe is likely to become increasingly whiny, move about looking for novelty, disturb other people, and end up being spoken to sharply by them or by Mom and Dad. Make-believe provides a set of tools that are useful in many situations, and it is a valuable means of dealing with loneliness or confinement.

Creativity

Creative adults and children are blessed with a keen awareness of both the internal and the external worlds. They are extremely responsive to their body states, and are attuned to the details of their envi-

 FANTASY AND PRETEND PLAY CAN TRANSFORM A DULL OR TEDIOUS SITUATION INTO SOMETHING FUN.

ronment, including its sights, sounds, and smells, and its objects to touch and explore. Make-believe opens children up to the curiosity, novelty, and originality that so enrich all human existence, and increases their ability to explore new contexts and try out new situations in fresh combinations.

Exploration of novelty makes children sensitive to the creativity of others, as expressed in stories or movies or art, and lays the groundwork for their own creative development. Research shows that men and women who demonstrated creative achievement early in their adult lives had engaged in a good deal of fantasy as children and often developed imaginary companions. They were also exposed to considerable storytelling by their parents, or had played pantomime games with them.

Creative living implies much more than the production of literature or art. Our lives as adults are full of opportunities to express originality and creativity. The mother who quiets a temporarily frightened or uncomfortable youngster by diverting her with little make-believe games, rather than by shouts or threats, is showing a simple yet valuable form of creativity. A young man may be trying to break into a career field that is highly competitive; by playing out in his mind's eye several possible ways of attracting the attention of executives in that field, he may decide that an investment in a trade magazine advertisement could lead to dozens of interviews and contacts. By taking a situation that is distressing or frightening or frustrating, and twisting it imaginatively—even carrying it to an absurd fantasy—one can lighten one's mood for a moment or discover a different and effective way of coping with difficulty.

CAN MAKE-BELIEVE BE DANGEROUS?

Some parents may worry that make-believe will confuse their children's ability to distinguish between reality and fantasy, or encourage them to withdraw emotionally. A few dramatic cases described in the psychiatric literature do involve children who have spent an excessive amount of time playing fantasy games or developing imaginary kingdoms. The danger, of course, is that the child may come to so enjoy the world he can control alone that he avoids the necessity of dealing and interacting with other children.

Fortunately, however, excessive withdrawal into fantasy is extremely rare. In fact, most research on the behavior of children who eventually show serious emotional or social difficulty indicates that the children most prone to such problems are extremely active, often directly aggressive or obstreperous, and most significantly for our purposes, relatively undeveloped in terms of their inner lives. In short, more imaginative children are less likely to evidence breakdown or distress.

For the parent or teacher who is concerned about how much fantasy life is too much, the answer is pretty simple. If a child has withdrawn so completely into the world of make-believe that his learning of simple skills suffers drastically, he has no child companions, and his personal habits have become sloppy, then professional help should be sought.

But the risk of such developments is far less than the risk to children who fail to make sufficient use of their imaginative abilities. These are the youngsters who are more likely to run into serious problems in society. They often show great difficulty in dealing effectively with the anxiety and stresses that are inevitable parts of growing up. When a child's range of make-believe is too limited, he is more likely to focus on extremely narrow fantasies, leading to distortion of later reality. Sociodramatic play—pretending to be other people in various social roles—is really preparation for facing complex realities, and a child's imaginative anticipation of numerous situations prepares him or her to respond effectively to these realities.

CAN MAKE-BELIEVE BE TAUGHT?

Many notable and creative persons in the arts and sciences often enjoyed early contact with an adult who directed their imagination along a particular line and played a key role in their development. For example, playwrights George Bernard Shaw and Johann Wolfgang von Goethe played with their cherished puppet theaters, inventing stories to fill their childhood days, with the interested encouragement of their mothers.

In the simple make-believe play of nursery school children, research indicates that an adult can be important in changing the pattern of make-believe play that a child exhibits. In our own research with a nursery school group on the effects of a television program on children's play, the greatest increase in spontaneous make-believe play came when the children's teacher engaged in entirely make-believe games and encouraged them to try, too.

Also, our research showed that a carefully produced television show increased make-believe play in young children, but only if an adult sat with them during the show, encouraged them to pay particular attention to some of the material, and when it was over, helped them try out some of the imaginative possibilities. The children who watched television without any adult intervention at all showed the least increase in make-believe skills. It is clear that a parent or teacher can be of tremendous value in enhancing the imaginative capacities of their children.

Even in the first year of life, face-to-face contact with a smiling, interested, softly speaking adult is a tremendously important experience for the child. Throughout the early years the child needs the smiles, pleasant speech, and playful reactions of a familiar adult—a mother, father, aunt, teacher, or baby-sitter. That smiling face helps the child develop a sense of someone else out there, which encourages a sense of both self and others. Children begin to try to imitate the adult's facial expressions, words, and gestures, and out of this imitation, they shape the plots for their first make-believe games. An adult can help the child develop her imagination further by playing little games with her. A teddy bear or stuffed animal hidden under a chair or behind a sofa, or a game of hide-and-seek, can be very exciting to a two- or three-year-old.

For the three- or four-year-old, a parent can choose some of the "outside" people who so fascinate young children—police officers, auto mechanics, fire fighters, supermarket cashiers, television personalities—and encourage the child to pretend that simple playthings represent these individuals. Quiet moments alone with a child can turn in to extremely important learning times when there is a playful interaction between adult and child. This can be accomplished casually and with spontaneity.

COMMON MISTAKES THAT INTERFERE WITH IMAGINATIVE PLAY

In our experience, problems can result when children are always occupied with organized activities. Maintaining too many lessons or defined tasks can be exhausting for everyone, parents and children alike. Daycare centers and nurseries may keep youngsters almost too busy. From age two-and-a-half on, many children attend school for at least part of the day. And for somewhat older children, there are sometimes too many formal after-school programs.

Instead of unscheduled games of ball, kids now confront leagues dominated by parents, who are sometimes fiercely competitive. Recall the "Peanuts" cartoon in which Charlie Brown learns with his characteristic wistful bewilderment that even making snowmen in winter has been organized as a little league by the parents! We encourage parents and teachers to strike a balance between structuring children's activities and giving them a chance to play on their own. Our intention with this book is to suggest ways in which par-

ents and teachers can foster play skills that will make children better able to enjoy time on their own, free of adult supervision.

Some parents believe that television is a stimulant for imaginative play. It can be very useful, but only under special conditions (see chapter 10, "Using Television for Imaginative Growth"). Too often television becomes a baby-sitter, with children plopped in front of it so that busy parents can go about their chores. The prepackaged fantasies of television cannot help children develop enough of their own skills to fill quiet time. It is very easy for children to become dependent on the outside stimulation of the tube instead of relying on their own capacities.

Children are best served when they can develop a skill, initially with adult help, that they can soon exercise independently, free of outside intervention. When adults offer consistent encouragement of make-believe skills, children become able to move off on their own, creating lively and exciting new environments for themselves. And these skills, which research indicates are well-established in some children by four years of age, can serve throughout life as a reservoir of personal resourcefulness, liveliness, creativity, and self-esteem.

The teacher or parent thus has a critical role in the child's development of play skills. Ideally, the adult encourages imaginative play and conveys to the playing child a sense of involvement and emotional warmth once a game is started. Then, once the game is under way, the adult steps back and allows the child to pursue his own direction, at his own pace.

Research has demonstrated that parents who intrude on their children's play are less successful in fostering imagination in their children than are parents who simply help their preschoolers start a game and then leave them to their own devices, interacting only on the child's initiatives. When the child can follow her own initiatives, an exciting and lively interchange usually takes place between parent and child around an increasingly imaginative and complex story line. Adult contribution is critical, but after showing the child the excitement of play, the most effective adult avoids dominating the game or organizing the play too much. The reward is watching the child bloom in the spirit of the game.

OUR APPROACH TO MAKE-BELIEVE

This book features a series of approaches to make-believe play with preschool children. The exercises and games can be carried out by parents at home with their own children, or by nursery school teachers or daycare center staff members. They are devised to encourage a wide range of skills—including motor, language, and problem-solving—while helping children learn to play with their peers. And they are a source of delight to both adult and child.

Although this book is primarily about preschoolers, play is important for older children, too. Eight-, nine-, and ten-year-olds still use bits of sticks or cards to represent favorite baseball heroes in a board game and dress dolls to resemble make-believe heroines. Acting in a school play or participating in a social studies project that involves dressing up in costumes of foreign lands is a welcome carry-over from the sociodramatic play of early childhood. Older elemen-

IF IT'S NOT FUN,

IT'S NOT PLAY.

tary school children and adolescents often spend time daydreaming or envisioning themselves in numerous grown-up roles; these inner fantasies are a helpful technique for passing time in waiting rooms, on long car rides, while performing household chores—any other situations that would otherwise be boring.

Children can play with adults in many ways. Obviously, girls and boys learn a great deal from playing checkers or athletic games with their parents, and from mastery activities such as building with blocks and other materials. The purpose of this book is to guide parents and teachers to the next step in the course of such play: accepting and encouraging the make-believe elements that children add spontaneously to these games.

A note of caution: Although the activities in this book can be used with children between the ages of two and five, it is important to remember that these three years are a period of great change and growth. The two-year-old has a small vocabulary, limited motor coordination, and very little concept of time or space, different colors, numbers, and other abstractions that older children are well versed in. As such, take care not to present a child with a game that is too far beyond his abilities. A little stretching of the mind is a fine thing—that's how children pick up the new ideas that they then attempt to use during imaginative play. But be alert to the fact that for the two-year-old, notions of color, complicated story plots, and so forth are merely confusing, and that any given preschooler may not understand commonplace phrases or have a grasp of metaphor. For a three-year-old, for example, someone described as "a pretty sharp fellow" may be imagined as someone who bites!

Play may be the main business of childhood, but if it's not fun, it's not really play. Recognize those moments when you may be pushing too hard, and ease off. A smile, a laugh, a kiss, and a quick shift of direction can make all the difference in the world by helping the growing child to best use what you are offering.

Finally, accept that a young child cannot easily grasp the subtleties and difficulties that lie between a wish and its fulfillment. The very young child jumps from the "stick 'em up" of the bandit cowboy toy to its capture by the sheriff on a miniature horse in one quick swoop. This omnipotent or "magical" thinking is often considered a basic feature of children's thoughts. But the magic also conveys the child's sense of mystery and wonder about what is strange and new, an interested awe that is one of the most precious experiences we can have. The daydreams of adults can also have some of that magical quality, yet too often we dismiss this side of ourselves. Helping children develop and expand their ability to make believe may help keep that sense of magic alive for them throughout their lives. §

CHAPTER TWO

What Make-Believe Can Do for Grown-ups

Parents and teachers who play the make-believe games outlined in this book with their children will likely discover that something is beginning to change in themselves. In reaching out for the child through empathy and imaginative play, they may easily find themselves coming back into contact with long-forgotten fantasies, wishes, and games, hidden in secret recesses of memory like the little private hideaways under stairs, in attics, or in woodland groves that children love so well. This chapter offers adults various approaches to recapturing some of their own early childhood play experiences. As you go through the activities, you will find yourself enjoying your own increased imaginativeness as you gain new ways of stimulating your child.

Adult "playfulness," as described by American author and play

specialist J. Nina Lieberman, can be a useful asset in turning dull routines into more pleasurable experiences. A roofer working on another ordinary house pretends he's repairing the roof of a famous theater, or takes time out to note a bird or an unusual tree. A commuter on her way to the office pretends she is an alien from another galaxy, seeing the earthly buildings and roads along the way for the first time. Teachers and shopkeepers, accountants and dentists, plumbers, lawyers, auto mechanics, and everyone else engaged in the usual business of daily living can find chores less humdrum by using their imagination and maintaining a sense of humor.

MEMORIES

One way to open yourself to playing with children is to look back on your own early days. We tend to forget much of our childhood once it is past—the little private games we had, the secret societies, the magical rhymes we repeated, the ritual gestures we used to ward off bad luck, or our scary fantasies about the old house down the street or the old lady living there, who might be a witch or a fairy god-mother. Getting in touch with pictures, events, and fantasies of your childhood can increase your sensitivity to children's thinking and points of view, and may suggest new games to play and rhymes to teach as well. It may also help you enjoy again some of the delights of childhood or see yourself, as an adult, in better perspective.

Think back on activities and memories like these. Begin by relaxing in a comfortable chair or on your bed and trying to imagine your three- or four-year-old self again. A great deal of the so-called forgetting of childhood experiences occurs simply because we are never in the right place and time to arouse such memories. But once you say to yourself, "I'll lean back and be a child for a few moments and let my mind wander," you may be surprised by all the memories that filter through.

Hypnotic age regression—in which a hypnotized individual is required to "become," for example, a three-year-old—is simply a more extreme form of concentration that enables memories to flow back. You can accomplish this effectively by yourself, without hypnosis, by relaxing, trying to recall some of the body postures you liked as a child, letting yourself feel like one for a moment, and seeing what images of early times come to mind.

With practice, you'll find that dozens of delightful experiences, wishes, and daydreams will emerge. You may want to repeat some of these with your children, both to re-experience the pleasure yourself and to pass on the joy to another generation. In either case, you'll have the opportunity to share your past and connect with your child on an emotional level.

On the other hand, some memories will not be pleasant. Teasing, cruelty, and threats have always been part of childhood, too. You may remember that your older sister dragged you to the bath-

GETTING IN TOUCH WITH YOUR CHILDHOOD MEMORIES CAN INCREASE YOUR SENSITIVITY TO CHILDREN'S THINKING.

room and threatened to flush you down the toilet, or recall an uncle who used to "pull off" your nose and show it in his hand by slipping his thumb between the fingers of his clenched fist. Or worse. Although your children or those you work with may not have endured the most painful forms of teasing, they are still vulnerable to many fears and doubts, and your own sad or painful memories can help you be more sensitive to what a child is going through.

Your own memories can help you be more sensitive in other ways, too. You can see, for example, how make-believe games of danger and adventure help children gain a sense of control or mastery over the many "real" dangers they believe surround them. You can also try to get in closer touch with your child's world. Look at the toys, furniture, and setting. Think about music that the child likes. Watch the ebb and flow of your child's play, alone and with other children. You will be surprised at how much more closely you sense what your child goes through from day to day. This, in turn, will increase your playfulness with him or her.

DREAMS When we go to sleep at night, we are treated to a night-long picture show full of fascinating twists and turns, vivid scenery, and the reappearance of long-forgotten friends and relatives. Dreams reflect some of the most creative capacities of human beings. You can take advantage of the novelty and even the peculiarities of these natural experiences to give you ideas for stories that you can adapt for playing with your child.

Although many people believe they never dream, laboratory research indicates that thinking goes on through most of the night for everyone. It's just that some people remember their dreams better than others do. You can train yourself to remember dreams by the simple process of keeping a dream log or diary. Place a notebook and pen by your bed, and a flashlight if you don't want to switch on the

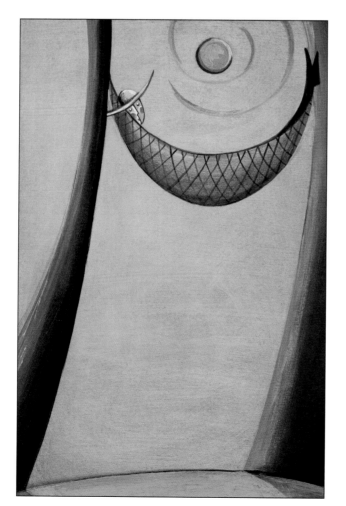

bed lamp. If you awaken during the night, write down quickly and briefly the main points of the dream you just had. Do the same thing on awakening in the morning. The best technique is to lie still for a few minutes upon awakening, playing and replaying the dream pictures in your mind. Then write them down. If you do this for a month, you'll find that your recall has improved dramatically—and you'll have an impressive and intriguing collection indeed.

The object of the dream log is not to look for the symbolic interpretations that are used in psychoanalysis. However, if you keep track of the main characters, the major themes, and the occurrence of certain motives such as achievement, power, sex, desire for closeness, and aggression, you will also notice facets, trends, and directions in your personality, activities, and intentions. This awareness can make you more sensitive to other people and to their emotions and motives. The novelty of your own dreams can also help you appreciate the beauty or humor of modern art, fiction, and movies. At the same time this sensitivity is helping you personally, it will deepen your awareness of the kinds of material your children enjoy in stories, movies, and television.

Keeping track of your night dreams can help you separate realities from fantasies, enhancing your understanding of how hard it may be for a child to make that kind of separation. The young child, under the age of three or four, cannot always tell in the morning that

DREAMS REFLECT SOME OF THE MOST CREATIVE CAPACITIES OF HUMAN BEINGS.

a night dream was not an actual event. You can explain that dreams are make-believe trips we make at night in our heads, like the make-believe games we play with our blocks and dolls and toy cars and planes by day. In this way, you help the child gain a sense of separation between night dreams and reality, and you avoid dismissing the inner reality of the dream.

Brian Sutton-Smith, a leader in play research now retired from the University of Pennsylvania, has developed the theory that play or make-believe gives the little child a feeling of power in a world of people and objects so much larger than he or she is. In a sense, being able to label our dreams as dreams and to see them as emanations of our own brain can give adults, too, a sense of power and control over what often seems mysterious and alien.

The Senoi tribe in Malaysia, which has been studied extensively by the British anthropologist Kilton Stewart, takes its dreams seriously. Within a Senoi family, dreams are recounted between parents and children every morning. Stewart believed that this practice plays an important role in the Senois' apparent tranquility and freedom from emotional stress and violent conflict. Whether Stewart's belief is true or not is a question for research, but certainly the friendly exchange of dreams around the breakfast table can introduce a sense of warmth, release, and openness to creativity for parents and children to share. Parents might try this dream sharing as part of an overall effort to use playfulness to build rapport and communication within a family. Teachers, too, could encourage such a morning sharing now and then. Of course, many dreams involve danger and distressing situations, or open sexuality, so parents and teachers should proceed with a measure of caution.

FANTASIES

Almost everybody daydreams from time to time during the day and just before dropping off to sleep at night. Indeed, daydreams are a normal manifestation of the way the brain works to store the vast amount of information it accumulates, and we believe they represent basically the same physiological process as night dreams. You can thus approach your waking fantasies with the same spirit of playful sensitivity as your nocturnal daydreams.

Because daydreams occur when we are awake, using our senses and muscles to deal with the external environment, they seem less vivid. They also are restrained from too much oddity by our conscious awareness of the physical reality around us. Nevertheless, our daydreams often carry us far away, and they suggest recurrent yearnings—the major unfinished business of our lives. When used with discretion, they can be rich sources of ideas for games and make-believe activities for children.

Discretion is important, because our waking fantasies are often for mature audiences only. In daydreams we might explicitly wish for sexual power or sexual explorations with friends' spouses or our co-workers, or weave stories around our jealousies, envies, and greed. (In night dreams such themes are often disguised or represented symbolically.) In a word, parents should not use their children as confidantes. This can be dangerous, placing too heavy a burden on youngsters who lack the perspective and emotional stability to cope with

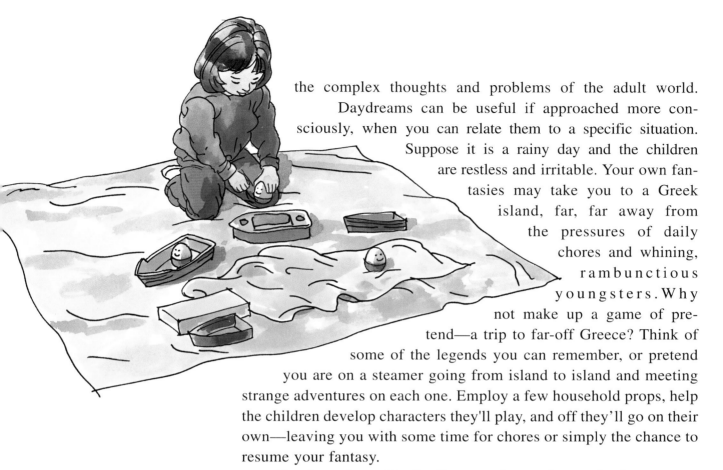

the complex thoughts and problems of the adult world. Daydreams can be useful if approached more consciously, when you can relate them to a specific situation. Suppose it is a rainy day and the children are restless and irritable. Your own fantasies may take you to a Greek island, far, far away from the pressures of daily chores and whining, rambunctious youngsters. Why not make up a game of pretend—a trip to far-off Greece? Think of some of the legends you can remember, or pretend you are on a steamer going from island to island and meeting strange adventures on each one. Employ a few household props, help the children develop characters they'll play, and off they'll go on their own—leaving you with some time for chores or simply the chance to resume your fantasy.

Daydreaming adds liveliness, color, and even intrigue to our lives. It helps us become more creative in our work and in our social relationships. It can help us plan for the future, when we pay attention to our fantasies and ask ourselves whether some practical steps toward fulfillment of these yearnings are possible. We can even use our daydreams to calm ourselves. Many psychotherapists and researchers in biofeedback report that picturing yourself in a peaceful, natural setting can have a very relaxing effect when you are anxious or angry.

Taking a cue from the imaginary companions our children create, we can sometimes overcome the ache of loneliness by engaging in mental conversations with friends or relatives, or even our own simulated characters. In Saul Bellow's novel *Herzog*, the hero writes mental letters to famous people: "Dear Winston Churchill—," "Dear General de Gaulle—." An approach like this not only eases loneliness temporarily but also may stir us into action, writing actual letters and enjoying the increased contact this generates. Bring your child into this by writing letters to grandparents together or by composing messages to send to the pumpkins at Halloween.

Memories, dreams, and fantasies are rich inner resources that adults can draw on to develop their playful capacities. In addition to looking inward, you can enhance your playfulness by watching children and playing with them. There is much to be learned from observing how a child tries to cope with the complex environment he or she confronts. The late Massachusetts Institute of Technology psychologist Kurt Lewin captured the fancy of behavioral scientists the world over in the 1920s with his charming movies of a toddler trying to sit down on a chair. We take for granted that to sit down, one turns one's back on the chair and eases into it. But as Lewin's films showed, for the one- or one-and-a-half-year-old toddler, turning your back means

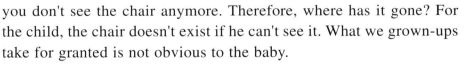

AS A PARTNER IN PLAY WITH A CHILD, YOU ARE LIKELY TO LIVE A RICHER LIFE.

you don't see the chair anymore. Therefore, where has it gone? For the child, the chair doesn't exist if he can't see it. What we grown-ups take for granted is not obvious to the baby.

Watching your child struggle with problems like these can help you gain perspective, not only on what he or she confronts daily, but possibly on some of your own approaches to situations in your life. You empathize with children's curiosity and delight as they explore. You can ask yourself whether there isn't much that you too can find out if you bring the same attitude of curiosity and wonder to what you do. Watching closely will also help you decide when to intervene and when to keep away. A good rule is that tasks should have some challenges. Frowns or tears are soon past, and the child moves on in the game or exploration with a greater sense of competence. If you intrude on the process too soon, you'll only encourage dependence.

Playing with your children can be exhilarating. It means putting aside daily cares and worries for a little while and living the gaiety and wonder of the stories and games you work out together. Down on the floor in the doll corner or the pioneer village, you can recapture your past innocence. Simultaneously, you can cherish the thrill of being an adult still capable of fun and excitement. And you can rise from the experience afresh, with a new sense of lightness and delight. In our own work, we have often observed that therapists who work with children, or kindergarten teachers or parents who enter the game from time to time, have a warmth and vitality that more sober adults with little involvement in children lack. As a partner in play with a child, you are likely to live a richer life.

BEFORE YOU BEGIN

The readers of this book may be fathers, mothers, grandparents, baby-sitters, kindergarten teachers, daycare center or nursery school teachers or aides, or simply interested adults. Each has a key role to play with children as an onlooker, a participant, or a stimulator or teacher of play behavior. Let us take a closer look at how adults can play with children.

One of the greatest pleasures of being a parent or teacher is the sheer joy of watching a young child grow. In the years from two to five, the child unfolds in enchanting complexity, changing from a baby to a searching, curious, emotionally vital, and imaginative being. Given a fair chance, most children show this wonderful expansion of intellect, imagery, and sensibility. The exercises and parent or teacher interventions in this book will abet and sustain these great possibilities of growth. While childhood is neither naive innocence nor a blissful golden age free of conflict, it does have a quality of playful invention that many adults have lost or mislaid. One important benefit of working with children is the chance it gives grown-ups to recapture that miraculous sense of wonder, exploration, and subtle power over the routine world.

Preschool and kindergarten children welcome an adult as initiator of a game. Most of them have not yet developed a significant store of different story lines or themes, and they are hungry for ideas. You can begin by telling or reading a story, or by gathering a set of toy soldiers, utensils, toy cars, and planes or blocks. The child needs some structure at the outset, so you might limit yourself to only one story or game of bus trip and to one special room with a certain set of toys. Children welcome enthusiasm—"This is going to be a really exciting story!"—and other evidence of adult involvement. Convey to the child as concretely as possible the events in the make-believe plot or story you are reading. Let yourself go when you imitate train whistles, or Martian voices, or the heroic tones of the captain of the spaceship. The child learns a great deal from such variations in speech and also is delighted by your efforts.

Plan to look over books and tapes such as those suggested in the appendix on pages 168-174 either before you begin the play exercises in each chapter or as you carry them out. Thus, you might read the book *Tibby Tried It*, by Sharon and Ernie Useman, before you begin the animal games. You can also invent your own stories for the games we suggest; the appendix is merely a starter. The most important tools for a parent or teacher to have on hand are, first, the desire to participate as an imaginative partner with the child, and second, a readiness to use everyday materials imaginatively.

Above all, enjoy the games. Whether parent or teacher, your enthusiasm and joy will be contagious and will invite your children to become your willing partners in play. You will also be training them in a subtle way to use play on their own and with other children.

As you watch children move from the role of Peter Pan or Wendy to a cruel pirate or to Tinkerbell and then back to their own selves in the blink of an eye, you can't help but admire the fine line they can walk between reality and fantasy, the magical thinking that enables them to play out numerous scenes that cross back and forth in space and time. The capacity to experience mystery and wonder in the face of what is new and strange is one of the most precious qualities we as humans possess. As parents and teachers of these very young children, you have the opportunity to help them develop and expand their capacity for make-believe and keep that sense of magic alive throughout their lives. §

FOR PARENTS

Each of the following chapters contains a discussion of the specific benefits your child may gain from the type of activity that is the chapter's focus—motor, sensory, role-playing, watching television. Try to start with the activities with which you feel most comfortable. As you play, you will become more experienced with the process. You might want to think of the kind of stimulation or a particular growth area in which your child needs help. The discussion of benefits at the beginning of each chapter will help you identify a good match between your child and the games and activities suggested.

Children differ enormously in their patterns of interests, their motor and language skills, and their initial responses to certain games and activities. For this reason, the book is not structured by age. The general age group that is most likely to enjoy or understand a particular game or activity is often suggested, but usually the games can be modified to work well with children at all age levels from two to five.

To keep the games fun for you and your child, you may want to start playing the simplest ones first. Watch your child to see if he is bored or restless. If so, stop. Try a more challenging game the next time. The goal is for you and your child to experience both pleasure and success. For this reason, it is best not to start with a game that may be too difficult. Once you feel comfortable with the simpler games, experiment with others that are suggested for a child older than yours. Also, try variations of the game using your own ideas and inventiveness.

Watching children is an art in itself. It is important to be able to step back and observe to learn about your child, and also to allow her to develop her independence and competence. One must take care to be unobtrusive, blend into the background, and avoid rushing out to help pick up fallen toys or smooth the edges of a block castle. In the home, the parent or other adult is usually keeping track of only one or two children, possibly with a visiting child or two as well. You can be busy with other things and still pick up a great deal from a child playing in a corner of the kitchen or play area. It is also easy to listen to children's chatter in the next room at naptime or bedtime and learn a great deal about their play themes and preoccupations.

Sometimes children will draw you into a game. Here the art—which may not be easy—is to maintain your adult status while going along with the game. To play at make-believe, you may have to unbend a little, imitate different voices or sound effects, or get down on the floor to avoid overwhelming the child by either your size or your better motor coordination. At the same time, you have to avoid acting too childish. A child is confused and distressed if she witnesses adults losing their dignity or behaving like a baby. Enter into the game with gusto, but try to play a somewhat more adult role—or at least one in which your size can be employed—as the captain of a ship, a large animal, or a friendly giant. Occasionally children, especially two-year-olds, get enormous laughs from watching an adult play a baby, but this should last only a short time, and you should always indicate to the child how funny the whole situation is.

FOR TEACHERS

A teacher, just as a parent, plays a critical role in the child's development of play skills. Children are best served when adults help them develop a skill that they can soon exercise on their own, free of outside intervention. When you encourage your preschool class to play make-believe games, they will soon create lively and exciting adventures by themselves.

It is best to play the games in this book with small groups of children. Although successful results can be obtained with half-hour daily sessions with as many as 15 or 16 children, optimal groups are closer to five or six in number. When you have extra help in the classroom, either an aide or a teacher-in-training, this would be an ideal time to take some of the children aside and engage them in one of the exercises.

It is important that the children be at approximately the same play level. One or two children who are not emotionally ready for group play and who disrupt the group by whining, or a combative child who breaks the flow of the game, can spoil it for everyone. Less concern need be felt about the occasional child who stays at the periphery and doesn't get very much into the game. Such a child may actually be absorbing a great deal and will reflect it in later play.

Many of the games contain concepts that children need for kindergarten, such as numbers, colors, shapes, vocabulary, and sequencing. They also contain ample opportunities for using good manners, such as saying "please," "thank you," and "you're welcome." As the children play these games, they will learn skills that can enhance their school readiness in a pleasurable way.

Playing with preschoolers should never become a chore or drill. As you know, the years between two and five involve great emotional sensitivity, strain, and growth. Children are developing not only vocabulary and motor abilities but also a sense of self and their complex emotional relationships to their mother, father, and siblings. Play can be quite useful in working through feelings of rivalry, jealousy, and self-doubt at these ages. Play also can help children develop a positive sense of self.

Begin with simple games and match the games to the capacities for your group. Don't play a game for too long a period. You want to avoid boredom. If the game seems too difficult and the children seem frustrated, stop and try another game or one that is shorter. Pick and choose the games from any chapter of the book. The beginning section of each activity will guide you concerning the props or materials you will need.

One way to get to know every child's level of play is by observing each individually during an unstructured play period. Note who is

a b c d e f g h i j k l m

the leader, and who seems isolated or shy. Who initiates the play? How often do the children change roles? Does one child dominate the play? Is there a child who stubbornly refuses to take on any role but the one favorite, whether it is a daddy, a monkey, or a superhero? Are there small groups of children who always want to play together?

For our own research projects, when we train students to be observers we emphasize careful attention to details, asking the students to write down almost every move the child makes and every sound or word uttered. Such thoroughness is necessary for interpreting the children's thoughts and behaviors most accurately. Once or twice you may find it useful to track a child through the playroom for ten minutes at a time to see if you can capture exactly what she does and says. Note the child's recurring speech patterns, play themes, signs of fear or hesitancy, and indications of just how her imagination is developing. If you want to intervene later, you will have a good sense of what places or games seem taboo for her, what phrases give her special delight, and what level of plot complexity is already developed in her make-believe play.

Once you have found patterns in the way the children play, you may want to use particular games for different children to help them expand their play activities and develop variety. Your role will be to stimulate the play by presenting the structure or outline of the game, offering novel ideas, and supplying some of the props. Try not to be too active, or the children will take a back seat and you will be the one doing most of the play.

See yourself as the guide who will keep the game moving if the children are stuck or get into squabbles with each other. You can help by asking questions, making suggestions, or modeling the play. If the children want the game to move in a different direction than the one you have in mind, be flexible and follow their lead unless the game becomes overly aggressive or completely disorganized. You can always present your ideas another day.

In some respects, the roles of teacher and parent differ. The teacher has many other children in her charge. She usually can't take the time to get into an extended make-believe game with only one or two children. The best tactic is to accede to a request to play by stating a time limit and suggesting other children who can later substitute for you. Also, teachers, even more than parents, should avoid taking too childish a role. Children in the four- to five-year age group expect their teachers to be even more distant and self-controlled than their mothers, fathers, and other adult members of the family.

n o p q r s t u v w x y z

CHAPTER THREE

Movement and Make-Believe

aby Karen is moving all the parts of her body almost simultaneously. Arms wave, feet stretch, head turns, eyes search, fingers grope for the mouth. She is in constant motion. Gradually, she will gain control, and her movements will become less aimless. The hand that seemed to move at random will reach toward a mobile or grab a rattle. With Karen's realization that this moving hand belongs to her and that use of the hand is now in her control, wondrous new possibilities will open up. Shiny objects can be grasped, sucked on, chewed, smelled, and dropped.

By the time a baby is ready to sit up, at about six months, everything in sight is a source of curiosity and potential pleasure, waiting to be explored. Soon the baby will crawl, walk, and run. The random exploration of objects will become a more prolonged affair

gradually turning into play, peaking at ages three to five years. Preschoolers seem to have boundless energy and an unending curiosity. They seem never to sit still.

Some children move freely, gracefully, and rhythmically, and others are more inhibited about using their bodies. While Diana seems almost to dance as she runs, Steven moves haltingly and self-consciously. Both are normal. This chapter presents exercises geared toward helping all children feel at ease with their bodies when moving and playing imaginative games. Children who develop control over their bodies become coordinated, agile youngsters who gain confidence as they master such skills as jumping, skipping, swinging, riding a tricycle, climbing, sliding, and running.

The imaginative activities that follow begin with finger games and lead up to larger movements involving the entire body. All of the games can be tried with all age groups, although you will want to stay alert to how much a younger child is capable of so that he does not become frustrated. Each of the exercises can be done with one child or with small groups, preferably three or four children at a time. In larger groups, it is more difficult to maintain each child's attention, and the children tend to vie for the leader's notice and become competitive. Ideally, both frustration and competition should be kept to a minimum, so that the youngsters can enjoy themselves fully and feel proud of their individual accomplishments. §

FINGER GAMES

Fingers become important to preschool children when they begin to draw, hold a pencil, start to tie their shoes, button their clothes, pull up zippers, feel textures, and of course, when they learn to count. Developing fine motor skills during the preschool years is helpful both now, as they begin to practice these tasks, and later, when they start school and continue to write letters, cut with scissors, paste, assemble puzzles, color designs, and put on their own clothing. Opening a milk container during snack time, cleaning a desk, writing with chalk, catching a ball, and countless other fine motor coordination activities, such as tying shoelaces, buttoning coats, and zipping up jackets, will become part of a child's daily repertoire of acts on the journey toward independence.

Finger Exercise

YOU WILL NEED:

- **play dough or modeling clay**

Seat the children around you at a table that has a washable surface. Set out non-toxic clay or play dough in small lumps. Let the children roll the clay into different shapes. Play music, if you like, to stimulate their creativity and pleasure. As you roll the clay, try reciting the following chant:

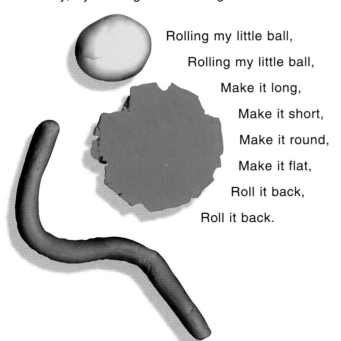

Rolling my little ball,

Rolling my little ball,

Make it long,

Make it short,

Make it round,

Make it flat,

Roll it back,

Roll it back.

Finger Counting

Fingers are handy for counting. Why not play some games that introduce numbers as your child exercises and plays with his fingers? Old chants and finger songs, such as "Five Little Blackbirds," make counting fun.

Hold up your hand to demonstrate so the children can imitate your finger movements. As you recite the chants, raise one finger at a time from a loose fist. It's easiest to start with the index finger and end with the thumb.

One little blackbird sitting on a tree,

Two little blackbirds,

And now there are three,

Here comes another one and that makes four,

Five little blackbirds fly through the door.

(Flutter all fingers and "fly away.")

One little doggy, he's all alone,

Two little doggies, chewing on a bone,

Three little doggies, scratching on the door,

Four little doggies, are there any more?

Yes, five little doggies, sleeping on the floor.

(Curl fingers back down.)

Finger Naming

Finger games are a good way to teach children the name of each finger. Have each child follow your lead in a little finger exercise like this. Use one hand at a time as you say the following:

> All fingers are closed and sleeping.
> *(Make a loose fist.)*

> Wake them up, one at a time: pinkie, ring finger, middle finger, index finger, thumb.

> After all the fingers are awake, let them go back to sleep: thumb, index finger, middle finger, ring finger, pinkie.
> *(Fold fingers down in reverse order.)*

> Sing softly while your fingers go to sleep, more loudly as you awaken them.

> Now use the other hand, too.
> *(Hold up both hands, in fists.)*

> Wake up all of your fingers.
> *(Name all ten, one at a time.)*

> Put all of your fingers to sleep.
> *(Name them, one at a time.)*

Repeat the exercise several times until the children learn the names of the fingers. Then ask each child to take another's hand or your own and wake up her partner's fingers as she names them, using one hand at a time, then both hands. Next, have the children touch one another's hands, naming the pinkie, ring finger, middle finger, index finger, and thumb on each hand. Once the children are familiar with the finger names, call for a finger to awaken out of order: thumb, pinkie, index finger, and so on.

Colored Rings

YOU WILL NEED:

- **yarn, at least five colors**

Let the children choose five short pieces of yarn in any color they want, and help tie "rings" on the fingers of one hand. Each finger should have a different color.

Say:

> All the fingers go to sleep.
> *(Fingers curl down.)*

> All red rings wake up!
> *(Finger with red ring points up.)*

> All blue rings wake up!

> All yellow rings wake up!

Hold up a piece of appropriately colored yarn with each command. This helps the child who doesn't yet know colors, and teaches colors as he learns to move his fingers. Note that each child will be waking up a different finger with a command. They will have to look at their own fingers, not at their neighbors', since one child's "red" can be a pinkie while another child's "red" is a thumb.

Finger Painting

YOU WILL NEED:

- finger paints in assorted colors
- finger painting paper or white shelving paper
- old cotton sheet
- curtain rod
- painting smocks, aprons, or old shirts
- newspaper to protect the floor

After playing the structured finger games described above, free finger movements, such as finger painting, make for a refreshing change of pace. Most children love the tactile sensation and the open-ended possibilities for expression that finger painting provides. For adults, an advantage of finger paints over watercolors and other media is that, at play's end, they wash off of skin and clothing easily. Use non-toxic brands for children.

FREE EXPRESSION
Each child should put on an apron or smock. Spread finger paint paper or white shelving paper over a table with a washable surface, and set out several colors of paint for the children to choose from. As they paint, urge the children to experiment with different techniques, including, in particular, making long, sweeping movements with the whole hand.

HANDPRINT MURAL
After this free-form exercise, you might like to try one that is a bit more structured. Spread out an old sheet on the table. You can make a smaller mural with a white cotton dishtowel, or a portion of a sheet. Put newspapers on the floor to protect it from drips and spills. Let each child dip his or her hand into a preferred color of paint so that the entire hand is covered. Next have the child make a handprint on the sheet or towel in whatever area he or she chooses. Help the children so that their handprints do not overlap too much, yet let them be free in arranging the prints to form a pleasing design all over the sheet or towel. When dry, the sheet or towel makes an attractive hanging for the playroom. Simply stitch a hem along one end, and slide a curtain rod or wooden dowel through the hem to mount.

FINGER MAKE-BELIEVE

Finger puppets combine finger exercise with creative expression, and are a marvelously interactive form of storytelling. They are especially good when a child has to stay in bed.

To make puppets, cut the fingers off of old gloves and decorate them with markers and other materials to look like people and animals. Use markers to draw features such as eyes, nose, mouth, hair or fur, whiskers, clothing, and so on. You can also tape or glue yarn, colored paper, fabric scraps, ribbon, and other materials that are safe for young children. Puppets may also be made of paper and tape to fit your child's finger. Make several puppets, and help your children develop skits such as those scripted on the next page. During puppet play, lead the way at first, and then let the child's imagination take over as much as possible.

YOU WILL NEED:

- old gloves
- markers
- scrap materials
- white or colored paper
- tape

The Cat and the Mouse

CHARACTERS:
cat finger puppet
mouse finger puppet

Pussycat goes to sleep.
   (Finger folds over and goes to sleep.)

Little Mouse comes along and says, "Squeak, squeak."
   (Mouse puppet is on the other hand.)

"Oh," says Little Mouse. "I can play all I want to now. Pussycat is sleeping."
   (Make the pussycat snore.)

Little Mouse suddenly starts to sneeze, "Katchoo! Katchoo!"

Pussycat wakes up and says, "Who's there? Aha! A nice fat little mouse! Here I come to eat you up!" Little Mouse runs away.
   (Finger moves behind your back.)

Pussycat says, "Well, well, no one is there. Time to go to sleep again."

Let's Be Friends

CHARACTERS:
boy finger puppet
girl finger puppet

A little boy is singing all alone, "I'm tall as I can be."
   (Stretch finger up.)

Then he sings, "I'm small as a tiny pea."
   (Fold finger down.)

A little girl is walking down the street and nods her head at the boy. "Hello! Hello!" she says, "Can I play, too? Hello! Hello! I'll play with you."
   (Girl is on separate hand.)

   (The two fingers can now be tall or small together, or try to wiggle, hide in the hand, and so on.)

Have You Seen My Dog?

CHARACTERS:
boy finger puppet
dog finger puppet
girl finger puppet

A little boy and his dog come out to play.
   (Puppets are on the same hand.)

The little dog runs away.
   (Finger is down and hidden.)

The little boy cries so much that a little girl hears him and comes to find out what's wrong.
   (Girl puppet is on separate hand.)

They look all around together.
   (Search all around the area, the room, or the bed if the child is ill, and make a big pretense of hunting for the dog.)

They find him!
   (Place the dog finger in amusing spots, such as under the rug, on a glass or cup, behind a chair, in the sink, or under the pillow.)

All three are so happy now.

HAND GAMES

Children gain a great sense of accomplishment when they learn to do things with their hands. These activities encourage integrated use of the fingers, foster hand-eye coordination, and introduce the concepts *right* and *left*.

Puppet Games

Hands can become anything the imagination wants them to be. As such, children enjoy using their hands for puppets. Most toy stores sell hand puppets, and they come in a variety of materials—plush fabrics, plastic, paper, and even rubber. You can also make your own out of old socks, paper bags, or gloves, and decorate them with markers, colored paper, ribbon, fabric, and any other scrap materials that are safe for use with young children. The ideal puppet collection contains both people and animals, and most children love to play with kings and queens, princes and princesses, and all manner of fairies, goblins, and monsters.

As they get engrossed in puppet play, particularly hero-and-villain themes, children often move out of the story framework and into quasi-violent interactions. They may use puppets to bump heads together, pretend to eat each other, or play fighting games. The alert teacher or parent can redirect some of these aggressive acts into a story that uses such behavior as part of a villain's character. As long as the children understand that the puppet games are make-believe and that we do not hit our friends, some of this aggressive play within the story context can be permitted.

Make puppet characters that appear in everyday experiences, including a police officer, fire fighter, mail carrier, bus driver, doctor, shoemaker, or supermarket cashier. Your puppets can even be vegetables and fruits. For example, invent a game of things that grow, such as carrots, apples, bananas, and potatoes. Children can puppet-play vegetables and fruits and tell how they pick each one, how it goes on a truck to the market, how they buy it, put it in a bag, bring it home to wash and clean, and then—the climax—they eat it! And because this is make-believe, they can start the game all over again with their puppets intact.

Hands Are Special: Things They Do

Ask your children to sit near you and tell you all the things they can do with either or both hands. Here's a chance for make-believe. Let's all think!

> hammer a nail
> bounce a ball
> stir chocolate milk
> throw a ball
> blow a horn
> thread a needle
> make a cup
> make traffic stop
> cut bread with a knife
> make birds fly
> cut paper with scissors
> open a jar
> make a tent
> make an "O"
> make a "V"
> wind a watch

Touch It!

Ask your children to sit in a circle around you, and instruct them to:

> touch your nose
> touch a button
> touch your toes
> touch a zipper
> touch a sneaker
> touch someone near you
> touch your hair
> touch someone's socks

Ask each child to think of something he or she likes to touch. Have him or her name it, draw it if possible, or perhaps act it out—it might be a favorite pet!

Right Hand, Left Hand

YOU WILL NEED:

- ribbon or yarn in assorted colors
- red and green construction paper or gloves
- pail
- small ball, such as a tennis ball

Most children begin to learn the difference between right and left when they start school, although some learn sooner. In helping a child differentiate between right and left, color is a useful tool because children usually know the names of colors before they learn direction. Thus, if colored ribbon or yarn is tied on their wrists, children can link the concept of color with handedness to learn right versus left. For example, tie red on the right wrist and blue on the left. Then say, "Raise your right hand, the red one" and "Raise your left hand, the blue one." If children know their colors, they soon connect the color with the correct direction. If they don't know their colors, they are not ready to play such games just yet.

TRAFFIC

As children make believe they are cars or bicycles circulating around a room or an outdoor area, one child plays a police officer. She wears a red glove on the right hand and a green glove on the left. If you don't have red and green gloves, the child can tape red and green construction paper to each palm. The police officer controls the "traffic" by saying "Left hand means go" and "Right hand means stop" as she lifts the appropriate hand. Children enjoy taking turns at this game, and they learn left and right at the same time.

ROLL THE BALL

All you need is a pail and a ball. Rest the pail on its side, and let the child roll the ball into it from varying distances. The rules are simple. The left hand rolls a ball, and the right hand rolls a ball. With each roll, you and the child say "left hand" or "right hand." Keep a score for each hand of balls that get into the pail. This is excellent for developing coordination as well as learning handedness.

Shadow Figures

YOU WILL NEED:

- lamp
- blank wall (or hang a white sheet)
- darkened room

In this classic game, the child holds his hands between the lamp and the wall (or sheet), and arranges his hands and fingers so that interesting shapes appear silhouetted against the wall. Teach children to make different animals with their hands by demonstrating with your own hands first. They will enjoy guessing what the animal is.

ANIMALS

Make a crocodile by placing one arm over the other and opening the hands wide, with the fingers pointed toward each other so that in shadow they look like teeth. Make a bird by linking thumbs and flap hands. Try your hands at dogs, snakes, rabbits, and elephants, too.

MAKE-BELIEVE CREATURES

Children can become quite inventive if you say, "Now do a make-believe animal. It doesn't matter if the animal is your very own idea. Just take your hands and invent a new kind of animal."

SOUND EFFECTS

They also enjoy making the animal's sound as they imitate its movements. To vary this game, one child can make a shadow figure while the other children make animal sounds to go along with it.

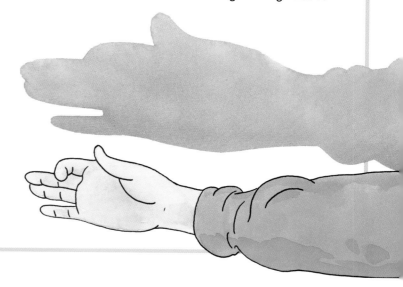

FEET AND TOES

Healthy, strong feet serve a child well in walking, dancing, and playing. These exercises for the feet and toes help strengthen the arches and muscles, developing balance and coordination.

Wiggly Toes

YOU WILL NEED:

- sandbox (outdoors)
- large box or old drawer, and plastic sheet (indoors)
- play sand

It feels great to wiggle toes—especially in sand. If you have an outdoor sandbox, let each child be barefoot and take a turn wiggling his toes in the sand, one foot at a time, then both together. If you live in an apartment, a shallow box filled with sand is a good investment. If you keep it on a piece of heavy plastic or oilcloth, the sand can be swept up and dumped back in the box.

Sand play (and water play, too) is so satisfying for the child that even the most meticulous parent might want to allot one small area of the house to "messy" play. If the child is given some simple rules about sand (and water) throwing and is held responsible for cleaning up with adult help, the joys can outweigh the inconveniences.

Tiptoes

Suggest that the children walk on their toes in a circle while you play a marching song, such as "Parade of the Wooden Soldiers." Encourage them to improvise. The uncomplicated beat of marches makes them especially easy to follow, but you can alternate marches with more imaginative rhythms, such as waltzes, rock-and-roll, folk tunes, and even classical music.

Toe-Shovels

YOU WILL NEED:

small, light objects for grasping, such as:
- plastic cups
- spoons
- clothespins
- small rubber ball
- wads of cotton
- soft washcloth

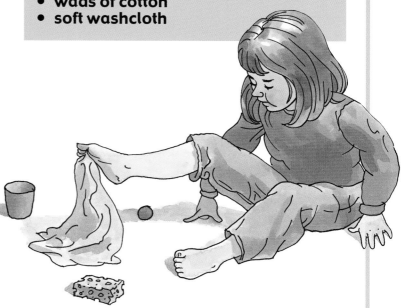

Place some small objects on the floor. Ask the children to make believe their toes are little shovels, and have them try to pick up the objects with toes only. It isn't easy, but you'll hear lots of giggling and laughter. With practice, children soon learn to pick up these objects and others, including those of their own choosing. You can play this game at any time in little snatches at home. For example, suggest that your child pick up a wet washcloth with her toes after her bath.

Feet on the Line

YOU WILL NEED:

- **chalk, or string and tape**

These two games are good for balance. Start by drawing a straight line with chalk on the floor or sidewalk. If you don't have chalk, string or a strip of fabric will do; indoors you may tape it to the floor so that it stays put.

CIRCUS TIME

Have the children pretend they are walking a tightrope in the circus. Show the children how to hold their arms outstretched to balance themselves as they:

> walk the "tightrope" on their toes
> walk with the whole foot
> walk backward
> hop

Younger children may not be able to walk backward or hop. Try to teach them, but move on to other games if they indicate that they are not ready.

BIRDS ON A WIRE

With older children, pretend to be birds hopping on a wire. The line needs to be long enough to accommodate several children at one time. Sing a little song:

> Hop, hop, here we go,
> Hop, hop, here we go,
> We are high in the sky,
> We are high in the sky,
> Watch us as we fly away!

Let the children fly off the "wire" and scatter about the room. Call them back and begin again.

Footprints

YOU WILL NEED:

- **modeling clay that dries hard**
- **finger paints**
- **large piece of heavy paper**
- **old sheet**

Feet are not just for moving from place to place. They can be a source of creative expression as well!

FOOT SCULPTURES

Make footprints out of clay by having each child step on a large enough piece of modeling clay to fit a complete, clear print. (Read the package label to make sure that the clay is non-toxic and that it hardens as it dries.) When you have a good impression, let the clay harden. The children can paint their own clay footprints with finger paint when they are hard and dry. Explain that they will have to wait a day or so before the clay is ready to paint.

FOOT MURAL

Footprints, like handprints, can also be made on a sheet. Each child dips one foot into a quantity of non-toxic finger paint placed on a sheet of paper on the floor, then hops—with your help—on the other foot to a nearby fresh sheet and stamps on it to make a footprint. Use as many colors of paint as you can manage, and scatter the children's footprints in any pattern. The finished sheet makes a cheerful playroom decoration.

Obstacle Course

YOU WILL NEED:

- cereal boxes
- empty carton large enough for children to crawl through
- large inner tube
- empty, clean cans (make sure there are no sharp edges)
- balance beam

A small obstacle course in the kitchen, playroom, child's room, or backyard is helpful for developing balance and coordination—and it is a source of fun and creativity.

The children can help you lay out the obstacle course in a large room or outside. You may want to alter the order of the obstacles on different days by rearranging the materials, but always place them in a large circle with enough space between objects for the children to maneuver easily.

1 Place several cereal boxes far enough apart so that the children can step over each one with ease. They can be arranged in a circle or in a straight line.
2 Next, the children crawl through a tunnel. Use the large carton, with both ends open. (Don't cut off the end flaps because this box can be your puppet theater or tea table at another time. Also, you may tuck them into the box for sturdiness.)

3 Next comes the balance beam, which can be placed alongside the tunnel or just after it. You may purchase a balance beam, or improvise one by placing a long block over two smaller blocks at each end, or several identical blocks end to end on the floor or ground.
4 Then the child moves to a circle made of spaced cans. The object is to tiptoe in and out around each can without knocking any over.
5 Finally, the children walk on the inner tube without falling off. The children will have completed the obstacle course by performing each of the five tasks.

Devise other obstacles as well, such as an overturned chair to crawl under or a small stepstool to climb up, with adult guidance. The children may have ideas of their own to try, too. Also, in the backyard, children can be more physically active if you set up an obstacle course with lots of space between each event, and perhaps hang a tire swing from a tree or posts. Be sure to use heavy cord, and hang it from a sturdy tree limb. Position the swing high enough from the ground to allow a little swing, yet low enough to permit a youngster to climb onto it and crawl through it without much difficulty.

If you play this game with several children, try timing each child's passage through the course every so often. Parents may also keep a record of their child's fastest time so that she may strive to exceed it. It's best not to time the children every time, since the prime objective is the pleasure of mastering a skill rather than winning a race. Try timing now and then if it suits the temperament of the children and their attitude toward competition.

Make-Believe Feet

Have the children take off their shoes. Describe the ways in which feet can let other people know how they feel, and act the feelings out with the children. For example:

walk fast across the room—*can't wait, eager, in a hurry*

walk slowly and drag your feet—*tired, sad*

stomp and jump hard—*mad, frustrated*

dance on toes and skip—*happy, excited*

walk on toes slowly, small steps—*careful*

step forward, step backward—*unsure, "I don't know," "Should I or shouldn't I?"*

ALL OF ME: THE WHOLE BODY

Children's bodies—like everyone else's—are designed to thrive with a certain amount of physical activity. It is well documented that physical exercise tends to result in happier moods, better memory, better sleep patterns, a sturdier immune system, and optimum energy levels. In addition, with childhood overweight and obesity now at epidemic levels, its health benefits are more important than ever. Children should therefore be given every encouragement to move their young bodies. One of their favorite action games is imitating objects and people.

Jack-in-the-Box

Have the children sit on the floor, and say to them:

Let's play jack-in-the-box.

Make believe you're in a little box.

Put your head down.

Cover the box—click goes the cover.

Tuck in your arms, and now your feet, so you make your self small in your box.

Now wind up your box and count to three—1, 2, 3—and out you pop!

Ready, back in the box, cover the box, make the lid tight.

Repeat the game several times, each time changing the count—to 3, to 5, to 4—that signals the children to pop out of the box. The added element of suspense makes the game more fun.

Body Exercises

These simple exercises combine stretching, bending, and other movements with imaginative play for a full mind-and-body workout. Gather the children around you, with enough room between everyone so that you can move freely. Give the following cues, and any others that come to mind, as you and your children act them out.

Bend over, catch ten little butterflies,
and say hello.
(Touch and grasp toes.)

Bend over, catch ten little leaves,
and then blow each one away.

Stretch up tall, reach the stars,
catch one if you can.
(Also use clouds, sun, rocket ships.)

Hop on one foot, like a little rabbit.

Jump, jump, jump, like a kangaroo.

Lie down flat, put your legs in the air,
and push that cloud away.

Skip to the store, buy some apples,
skip home again.

Lie down flat on your back and pedal
your bicycle.

Dancing

Most children love music. It can perk up a gloomy mood, ease tension, and inspire children to move their bodies in creative expression. Many, many recordings have been made especially for children to sing along with and dance to. When starting any dancing activities, some of these structured games may be better for the more inhibited child. "London Bridge," "Here We Go 'Round the Mulberry Bush," and "The Farmer in the Dell" are among the easiest movement games to learn.

When possible, though, encourage your children to invent their own dancing games. Suggest that they sit and listen first to the music. Then ask them to think about what the music sounds like; you might suggest a few visual images or feelings to stimulate their imaginations. Once their imaginations are involved in the music, encourage them to move along with it. Play music with distinctive styles, such as marches, waltzes, and even the tango. Also, alternate quick beats with slower tempos, and raucous music with softer, dreamier pieces.

As the children dance, tell them to make believe that they are:

a snowflake

rain falling down

leaves blowing all around

a goldfish swimming in a bowl

a firefly

a big stormy wind

a flag fluttering

smoke from a chimney

clothes blowing on a clothesline

a tree bending in the wind

a cloud moving across the sky

an ocean wave

CHAPTER FOUR

Living and Playing Through Our Senses

Imagery is our ability to produce again in our minds something we saw, heard, or otherwise sensed in the past, whether a few seconds ago, or months, or even years. Many people think of imagery as seeing *pictures* in the mind. It is true that the visual system is perhaps the most highly developed of all the human sensory systems. However, the other senses also play an active part in producing imagery. We have the capacity to reproduce sounds, smells, tastes, and touches as well as sights.

Imagery gives us a haunting power over time. We can suddenly recollect the smell of Grandfather's pipe and then recall how we loved to sit on his knee while he told a story. We can recapture in our "mind's ear" our mother humming holiday tunes, which recalls warm family get-togethers. The joy of living fully through our senses, the

taste of good food, the perfume of fresh flowers, the sight of red streaks against the deepening dark sky of a sunset—all are preserved for us by our ability to duplicate them in imagery. We savor life, tasting and re-tasting, seeing and re-seeing, by virtue of it.

To enjoy the benefits of imagery, children must first learn to use all of their senses. Experiencing sensations fully requires practice. It takes time for a sensation to develop adequately. If we shift too rapidly from one experience to another, we do not mentally store sensations in a way that permits us to recall them through imagery. Therefore, it is important that we help young children build up their sensing capacities in two ways: first, by exposing them to a wide range of sensory experiences, and second, by doing so in a focused, unhurried way that allows them to completely absorb the experience. When their senses thus become developed, imagery can be a delightful resource for recapturing pleasant sensations.

THE POTENTIAL OF IMAGERY

The potential we have for the full development of our senses is demonstrated dramatically by children who are born blind. These children have very vivid auditory imagery and can re-hear voices and sounds with greater detail and precision than the sighted person. They also have kinesthetic imagery to a great degree, enabling them to re-experience vividly movements they have made in the past, and to imagine the movements that others are making. And finally, their tactile imagery allows them to re-experience the feel of something soft or crinkly with a precision that the sighted person is less likely to have developed. In short, the skill the blind show in the development of their other sensory capacities points up the fact that most of us, relying heavily on our visual orientation, tend to neglect our other sensory channels.

Artists naturally develop their imagery strongly in the area of their medium of expression. One cannot doubt that Beethoven, for example, had remarkable auditory imagery, and that long after he became deaf he could hear sounds of beauty and power in his mind's ear, as evidenced by the music he composed later in his life. Beethoven had developed his hearing by practice. And so can children.

Imaginative play draws on the child's capacity for imagery— the train whistles he imitates, the transformation of a stick into an airplane. When children play make-believe games, they are both practicing imagery and perfecting their skill at it. Practice is key; repeatedly exercising the senses leads to richer perceptions both in real time and in memory. In essence, the development of optimal sensory awareness is the foundation of make-believe. As make-believe games become more complex, they make increasing demands on the child to introduce elements of sight, sound, touch, or movement imagery.

THE BENEFITS OF IMAGERY SKILLS

Interestingly, imagery skills and good vocabulary often go hand in hand. Research indicates that children who have well-developed imagery skills learn reading and vocabulary more rapidly. As we grow older, we then tend to rely more and more heavily on language to communicate and to think, but imagery remains as important as ever for effective thought, planning, and the enjoyment of life.

There is reason to believe that the purely imagistic aspects of our thinking are controlled more by the right side of the brain, while the logical, sequential, and precise thinking associated with language and arithmetic is governed by the left. Living fully in a complex world requires the ability to see mental pictures and recapture sounds or melodies, as well as the ability to summon up explanations and specific words for things. A person with both left- and right-brain abilities has the best array of tools for effective communication with others, for problem solving, for creative expression—in short, for optimal thinking. Therefore, it is important for children to have many opportunities to practice both feeling and thinking from an early age.

Children start to learn about the world around them through their senses. As parents well know, infants begin by exploring the world mainly through their highly sensitive mouths. Although infants can, of course, hear, touch, smell, and sense changes in body temperature even at birth, the finer, more subtle discriminations among the sense modalities appear somewhat later. The sensory games in this chapter are suitable for most preschoolers, although you may want to make slight adjustments based on a child's age. The goal is the full experience of sights and sounds, the smell, taste, and feel of things. These are the building blocks for the play castles of our minds. §

TOUCHING

From the moment she is born, a baby works at adapting to her environment. The sensation of touch allows her to have contact with people and things, and to learn much about the world around her. Children are natural explorers, and if they are given the opportunity to touch, their play becomes much more imaginative. The activities that follow encourage a child's tactile senses. In a world full of "don't touch" warnings, it is nice to be able to say "touch"!

Fingertip Sensations

YOU WILL NEED:

- **materials of varying textures**
- **shopping bag or fabric sack**
- **box or shelf**

TOUCHING BAG

Gather a collection of things with different textures, such as velvet, corduroy, feathers, cord, cotton balls, rubber, sticky tape, plastic, leaves, paper, cellophane, small stones or pebbles, knitted scarf, cork, bottle cap, lace, and burlap. Place these items one at a time in a bag, and have the children put their hands inside, eyes closed, to feel the item, describe how it feels, and if possible guess what it is.

TEXTURE SORT

Collect items that are smooth and rough, several of each texture. Ask the child to feel the items and sort them according to their texture. Repeat this game with other tactile categories, such as hard versus soft, damp versus dry, and so on.

MY FAVORITE THINGS

Keep a shelf or box of favorite things to touch. As the child finds an interesting object with a texture he likes, he can add it to the collection. Some of the items mentioned above could be kept in the box or on the shelf, such as bottle caps, feathers, and velvet.

Thermal Changes

Learning about temperature variations alerts children to the dangers of touching hot objects, as well as why they need to wear suitable clothing during extreme weather. In addition to this practical knowledge, children can begin to appreciate the fact that people in different parts of the world experience different temperatures and climates that, in part, account for clothing and housing variations. Some children are intrigued to discover places where it never snows, and places where it is always hot or always cold. In addition to the activites described here, you can also read stories about different climates and temperatures; several are listed in the appendix.

GETTING TO KNOW HOT AND COLD

Fill bowls with water from the tap that is hot, warm, and cold. Be careful that the hot water is not so hot that it could injure a child. Have the children touch the water and tell you whether it's hot, warm, or cold. Ask them how each of the temperatures makes them feel.

IMAGINE WHERE YOU ARE

Give the child an ice cube so that he can feel icy cold. Ask him to think of places where he would feel cold, such as:

> in the snow
> outdoors at night when the sun is gone
> near the air conditioner
> at the North Pole
> on an iceberg
> in front of an open refrigerator
> on the skating pond or rink
> wading in an icy mountain stream

Next, ask the child to think about places he could go to feel warm again:

> near the fireplace
> a sunny beach
> near the oven
> under a quilt
> near the radiator or heating vent
> near the clothes dryer
> in the sun
> in a snowsuit

Now have the child imagine places that are hot:

> the desert
> a spot too close to a campfire
> the inside of a car sitting in the sun
> the equator
> inside the oven

Last, talk about where he might go or what he might do to feel refreshingly cool again:

> wade in the ocean, lake, or stream
> stand near a fan
> stand near an open window when a breeze
>   comes through
> drink a cold drink
> wash his face with cold water or a damp
>   cloth
> go swimming
> walk barefoot in cool grass

MAKE-BELIEVE HOT AND COLD

Find pictures of hot and cold places and things. Images from magazines and travel folders from travel agencies are excellent. Have the children look at pictures of hot places and pretend to be there, feeling very warm. For example, make believe you are wiping off perspiration, make your posture limp and droopy, and walk very slowly.

Repeat with pictures of cold places, and make believe you are shivering and your teeth are chattering. Make believe you are putting on many layers of clothing, calling them out one by one as you go through the motions of getting dressed. Fold your arms across your chest; teach the children about the warmth of friction by rubbing your arms vigorously.

Look at pictures of hot and cold objects and talk about them. Discuss whether people should touch them. Ask the children how they would feel.

SMELLING

For many, the sense of smell is powerfully linked to memory. In the realm of smells, the newborn baby responds only to the strongest odors, but the young child can learn to tell the difference between more subtle smells—and react to them. Watch a toddler's expression when she smells something delicious, something pungent, something sweet, or something unpleasant.

Scent Box

YOU WILL NEED:

- **box or shelf**
- **small plastic containers with covers**

Set up a special area where you can share with your child a range of smells to experience. This could be a cardboard box that you keep in one place, such as a kitchen cabinet, or you might have a small shelf suitable for the purpose. Stock the box or shelf with small covered containers, and place a variety of ingredients in them, such as:

cinnamon stick	dab of perfume
cut garlic clove	prepared mustard
banana slice	peanut butter
dill sprigs	soap
coffee grounds	dandelion
onion slice	peppercorns
fresh ginger	drops of vanilla extract
teabag	pine needles
lemon rind	flaked coconut
rose petals	garden mulch
olive oil	baby lotion

With older children who have mastered the art of sniffing delicately, you can also use powdered substances such as ground spices and sawdust. (Younger children may inhale them.) Replace the items on a regular basis with new smells to experience, and be sure to empty perishable items from containers, unless of course you want your child to experience the odor of food gone bad!

As you and your children sniff the items in your scent box, enhance the experience by describing or reading or telling stories about each smell. You might also tell them about our noses and how our sense of smell works.

Nosing Out and About

On outings with children, call their attention to the smells around you. In the produce market, inhale the fragrances of a wide assortment of fruits and vegetables in season, such as oranges, licorice-like fennel, broccoli, earthy potatoes, bananas, onions, spicy radishes, and sweet peaches. Visit the herbs, too, and ask your child what the smell of basil or cilantro reminds him of. At the delicatessen or grocery store, sniff cheeses, spices, varieties of tea, and ground coffee. A trip to the park can yield new items for the scent box, such as dried leaves, a bit of damp earth, a berry, or a flower. A visit to the bakery and its marvelous smells of baking bread, rolls, cookies, and cakes is a fine way to top off the outing, especially if everyone gets a treat.

Kitchen Experiments

In the kitchen, parents and children can discover together how smells change during the course of meal preparation. Sniff individual items before combining them in dishes, sauces, and dressings; then smell the final concoction and talk about what is different. Smell a fruit such as a banana or mango before you peel it, and then after. Observe together how smells get stronger when foods that are cold or frozen are warmed up.

If you have a yogurt maker, children can learn about the change from mild milk to the more pungent final product. Add jelly or fresh fruit to vary the yogurt smell and taste, or add cinnamon or vanilla from the scent box and learn something more about transformation: spices smell strong when alone and less so when mixed in the yogurt.

TASTING

If a child begins to explore the world of taste at an early age, chances are the parent will be able to serve a wider range of foods with no fuss. Expanding a child's repertoire of welcome tastes may lead to better appetites and to a willingness to try new and exotic foods later on in life. And American psychologist Abraham Maslow even found in the 1920s that women who were open to a myriad of taste sensations tended to have high self-esteem and to be self-confident, strong, and self-assertive.

Varieties of colors and textures of foods also help the child form an appreciation for colors and textures that stretch beyond the food experience. Cut open a kiwi fruit, for example, and the glorious, glistening green may bring to mind a precious gem. The natural beauty of many foods has long been appreciated by the great cooks of the world, who are artists using both their eyes and their taste buds.

CAUTION!

Before beginning any tasting activity, make sure that your children understand that they must never put anything in their mouths unless their parent, teacher, or other caregiver has offered it. All poisons, insecticides, household products, cleaners, and medicines must be kept out of children's reach.

CAUTION!

If you use a tasting tray in the classroom, be aware of any allergies related to foods, such as nuts or chocolate. Obtain permission and allergy information from all parents before beginning any tasting exercise.

Tasting Tray

A tasting tray is probably the most fun of all sensory experiences, especially if you choose an assortment of things to eat that children find most luscious. Assemble bite-size pieces of several different foods on a tray or platter, such as:

> fresh fruits
> dried fruits, including raisins, apricots, dates, prunes, and apples
> mild cheeses
> dry cereals
> cooked macaroni and other pastas
> fresh or raw vegetables
> cooked vegetables
> bite-size pretzels
> bite-size crackers
> bread cubes
> pieces of baked goods, such as cake, brownies, and cookies

Put a blindfold over the children's eyes, and then bring out the tray. A blindfold should be a strip of soft fabric that ties comfortably behind the head and does not cover the nose or face. Help the children select one piece of food at a time, and have them guess what each item is. For older children, you may put together a tray with related foods, such as a variety of fresh and dried fruits.

An artfully arranged tasting tray is also a wonderful way to introduce foods of other cultures. Teachers may ask parents for suggestions based on the foods served at home, and then lead a discussion about different cultures and customs as the children sample the food. Parents and teachers alike can read stories aloud to set the scene for a particular country whose foods are being introduced.

Fun in the Kitchen

Children love to help with food preparation—and to eat the results. In the kitchen, allow children to assist within the limits of their skills, washing fruits and veggies, adding ingredients (which you may measure) and stirring them together, dropping spoonfuls of cookie dough on a baking sheet, and so on. Whenever possible, they should be participants rather than onlookers. This includes clean-up chores. Here are some suggestions:

- Bake cookies with the children, and have them sample ingredients that are safe to eat uncooked: sugar, spices, flour, and butter. Do not taste unbaked dough if it contains raw eggs. Eat cookies warm from the oven, and have another after they have cooled. Talk about the differences.

- Make applesauce together. Peel several apples, remove the cores, and slice them. Cook on the stove or in a microwave with a small amount of water until the apples are soft, adding more water as needed to keep them moist and to prevent scorching on the stove. Have the children taste the apples both before they are cooked and afterward. Add sugar and cinnamon to the cooked apples, and talk about the change in taste. Or divide the apples among several bowls and flavor them individually with a pinch of cinnamon, cloves, lemon juice, or brown sugar.

- When fresh fruits are in season, children enjoy making a fruit salad. They can touch, smell, and identify the colors of the various fruits as they taste them. Add lemon or orange juice, a pinch of sugar, or a little cottage cheese or mayonnaise to the salad for taste variety.

- Baking bread is also exciting. Children delight in seeing the dough rise and in touching it. Even if you use a bread machine, children can watch the kneading and rising of the dough, if the machine has a window, and smell its yeasty fragrance as baking begins. And of course, tasting the warm bread is the final treat. Try it plain, buttered, with jam, or with cream cheese for more taste variety. Sample store-bought breads, too, and have the children describe the differences.

- Most children love making and eating individual pizzas. Have them spread a spoonful of canned tomato sauce on an English muffin and top it with grated pizza cheese. They can set the mini-pizza on a baking tray for an adult to bake in an oven or a toaster oven at 350 degrees for 5 to 8 minutes. Talk about the difference in taste (and appearance) between the uncooked and the cooked cheese.

- Make fun faces by spreading peanut butter on a round cracker and decorating with raisins, nuts, cereal, and fruit to represent eyes, nose, and mouth.

HEARING

Very young children are fascinated by sounds: the tone of a mother's voice, the drip of a faucet, the hum of a motor, the crashing of thunder, the language of animals. As children learn to recognize and then re-create sounds, their tongue clackings become horses' hoofs and screeches substitute for sirens. Just as they learn to use words to communicate their thoughts, so do they use sound effects to communicate to themselves and others during pretend play.

From sound to music is a short step. By combining sounds in different ways, the child discovers rhythm, tempo, tone, and pitch. A melody may be created, and when words are added, a song is born. The fact that nonsense words delight as much as those with meaning only serves to underscore the power of sound itself. As children learn to coordinate the sounds from the environment with the movement and thoughts available within themselves, a world of possibilities opens up: They can move with the sounds, they can sing, they can find their ideas expressed through the music they hear, and they can create original music to express their ideas.

Do-It-Yourself Band

Set up an impromptu band, in which the children play xylophones, harmonicas, kazoos, or bongos, and have them make their own instruments too. Some suggestions are:

- Blow into an empty jug for a nice bass sound.

- Bang two pot lids to make noisy cymbals.

- Strike or rub two wooden blocks together for a nice hollow percussion sound.

- Lightly tap the inside of a small glass measuring cup with a metal spoon to make the sound of a bell.

- Tie metal spoons of varying sizes along a strong cord so they are able to dangle freely. Strike them with another spoon, and reproduce a glockenspiel.

- An old pot makes a good drum when hit on the bottom with a wooden spoon.

- Take the cardboard cylinder from a roll of paper towels, toilet paper, or wax paper, and paint it a bright color. This makes a delightful horn. A child can also paste streamers along its length or decorate it with stickers.

- Put a scoop of unpopped popcorn in a round oatmeal box, and tape the lid securely. This makes a nice gravelly sound when shaken.

Guessing Games

These games help to enhance a child's awareness of sounds by taking away—temporarily—his sense of sight. You will need to blindfold your children for these activities, or have them close their eyes. As in other activities, the blindfold should be a strip of soft fabric that ties comfortably behind the head and does not cover the nose or face.

WHO AM I?
This listening game can be played with a group of children. Blindfold the children or have them close their eyes, then situate them around the room. Touch one child's shoulder. The child who has been touched says, "Guess who I am," and the others try to identify his or her voice. If possible, give each child a chance to be "it." The children should be told not to disguise their voices.

WHAT AM I?

Blindfold your child or children. Have them try to identify a variety of household or classroom sounds, such as:

refrigerator humming
creaking door
door or window opening and closing
chair moving on the floor
toaster popping up
clock ticking
whistle
vacuum cleaner
water running in the sink
electric mixer
different musical instruments
chalk squeaking on a blackboard
brushing teeth

If you are playing with just one or two children, take them by the hand and lead them around the house or outside. Groups of children will need to remain seated while you create the sounds around them. They may need some practice in learning to recognize sounds, but soon their ears will become more sensitive, and the more they play these sightless listening games, the more they will enjoy recognizing other sounds they hear. Be inventive and try to find new sounds to listen to each day, both indoors and out.

Outside Noises

Take an outdoor listening excursion by going for a walk and calling out the sounds you hear, such as:

wind	walking on "crunchy" snow
a bird chirping	an airplane overhead
a car driving by	leaves rustling
a ball bouncing	dry leaves being stepped on
a dog barking	a twig being stepped on

Also, take listening excursions to different environments:

a school yard or playground,
a shopping mall,
a zoo,
a woodland area,
the ocean or seaside,
a city street

Recorded Sounds

Recordings of music, stories, and nature acquaint children with a wide world of sounds, stimulate a variety of body responses, encourage effective listening skills, and provide a repertoire of songs, all of which feed the imagination and promote make-believe play.

MUSIC

An extensive repertoire of songs and melodies is a great asset to a child. "I'll Race You Down the Mountain" may pop into a child's head as she mounts her tricycle; chants like "Abiyoyo" or "Zulu Warrior" can embellish adventure games; lullabies can be used to sing baby dolls to sleep; march music adds luster to a parade; folk songs express feelings and actions during play. Eventually children learn to add their own words to a familiar tune, and make up new tunes using old ones to guide them. The wealth of musical recordings available for children can help provide them with these tools (see the appendix for some suggestions).

Listen to different kinds of music and talk about them. Is the music loud or soft? slow or fast? happy or sad? Ask the children how the music makes them feel. Can the children identify which instruments are being played? Point out the sound of a piano, a drum, or a trumpet while you are listening.

STORIES

Listening to a story is a wonderful way to exercise the ear. Play the recording of a story (or read a book aloud), and talk about it afterward, asking the children questions about plot details, what they liked, how they felt, and so on.

NATURE SOUNDS

You can play recordings of wind, rain, waterfalls, the ocean, the jungle, and many other environmental noises. After listening to these recordings, look at pictures of the environments you've heard, and help your child imitate the sounds that go with them.

Animal Sounds

Young children love to imitate animal sounds. Have a "conversation" using some of these animal sounds:

cow	horse	pig
dog	lion	cat
rooster	sheep	monkey

Nighttime Sounds

Sounds in the evening often scare children. It can be both fun and reassuring for them to talk with you about the nighttime noises we hear, including:

a ticking clock
crickets
creaking stair
creaking branch
a pet moving about indoors
furnace switching on
buses and automobiles
refrigerator turning on
automobile horns
howling wind
sirens (police car, ambulance)
thunder
garbage trucks

Telephone

For this classic favorite, use two empty, clean frozen-juice cans from which one end has been removed. Make sure there are no sharp edges that could cut little fingers. Puncture a hole in the intact end of each can, large enough to pass a string through. Cut a piece of string, and push an end of the string through the hole in each can. Tie a knot at each end so that the string cannot pull out. Have the children paint the cans if they wish, and the "telephone" is ready for use.

While one child holds one can to her ear, another child (or an adult) speaks into the other can, enacting a conversation and experiencing the sensation of sound. Children enjoy testing the distance to discover the maximum efficiency of the sound travel. If permitted to experiment with distance, they will find that the telephone does not work if the string is longer than about 12 feet.

CAUTION!

Always supervise this game, and be sure to put it away when finished, as the string may pose a strangulation danger to young children.

SEEING

Games that focus on the eyes increase a child's awareness of the variety and subtle shades of colors, the infinite shapes, the range of sizes, and the countless other visual details of the world around us. The range of things to observe is limitless, and the objects you choose to highlight in the following exercises are up to you and your imagination.

Blind Man's Bluff

This classic game that all children love is a good beginning exercise to show children how much we depend on our eyes. Clear a room of obstacles and blindfold one child in a group. The blindfolded child has to tag another child to become the next "blind man." Instruct the children to walk rather than run, and to call out to the blindfolded child so that she can follow the sounds of voices.

Colors

Colors, of course, are one of the first visual concepts a child learns. In any of the seeing games in this chapter, we suggest that you refer to colors frequently.

Sometimes colors have specific meanings for children. In this so-called synesthesia, two senses are involved: the visual sense and another such as taste, smell, or hearing, which the child attaches to the color. For example, some children see red as "hot" or blue as "cold." Make this into a game by asking the children to associate objects or feelings with colors. In Mary O'Neill's *Hailstones and Halibut Bones*, "brown is cinnamon and morning toast" as well as "comfortable as love." Green is "lettuce and sometimes the sea" and also "the world after the rain, bathed and beautiful again." We have found that five-year-olds respond to these concepts and can become creative poets themselves.

Let the children be free to experiment with their senses and their colors. No one is ever incorrect in this game. Here are some suggestions:

- Suggest that the children think of blue and name all the things that smell like blue.

- Ask the children to tell you what red, yellow, and other colors mean to them. Such an open-ended question should yield some wonderfully surprising responses.

- Play music and ask the children to name the colors that the tune brings to mind.

- Have the children close their eyes, feel objects, and try to associate colors with them. For example, a cold glass of water may feel "white," or a piece of soft cotton may feel "brown."

- List their ideas on a piece of paper or the blackboard in preparation for making a color-meaning book. Use markers, crayons, or paint on a sheet of paper, one color per page. You might also use pictures in which a particular color predominates to represent the color. Along with the color, list the thoughts and feelings that the child associates with it. Each child can make an individual book that describes several colors, or in a classroom each child may choose one color to contribute to a joint book compiled by the entire group. Sometimes the color naming is more fun if it becomes a shared experience, with each child elaborating and adding to the others' meanings.

- Introduce children to the different colors of people's hair, eyes, and skin. Read a book such as *Bright Eyes, Brown Skin*, or play a tape such as *Free to Be...You and Me* (see the appendix).

Sightseeing Expeditions

Help your child develop a keener visual awareness of everyday things around the house, in the classroom, and outside. Look for items that can be used to delight the sense of sight and to learn about features such as color, shape, and size. Call them to the children's attention, and talk about their qualities. For example:

INDOORS

a bulb growing in a pot (measure it each week)

a kaleidoscope to see the changing patterns

colored glass (no sharp edges) to see how objects change color when viewed through it

identical items of different colors, such as sponges, spools of thread, or jars of paint

various pasta shapes, such as shells, bows, and elbows

a collection of different seashells

a collection of coins

the contents of a jewelry box

plants of various shapes, sizes, and leaf color

a toolbox

a spoon collection, including stainless tableware, plastic spoons, wooden cooking spoons, a ladle, and measuring spoons

a button box, with buttons of all shapes, sizes, colors, and markings

a mirror they have breathed on, making "clouds"

snowflakes on the windowpane

OUTDOORS

- clouds moving
- different flowers in a garden
- the parts of one flower
- plants that grow in the shade and plants that grow in the sun
- leaves blowing and falling
- different colored leaves in the fall
- things blown by the wind
- the parts of different houses, such as doors, windows, the roof, a porch, a garage, and number of levels
- acorns and pinecones
- the moon and stars
- a squirrel as it leaps from branch to branch
- birds flying in formation
- "steam" made by the breath in winter
- insects crawling and flying
- surfaces, such as sidewalks, streets, grass, playground wood chips, and water

Find It! dsign do around houf

Ask the children to sit in a circle and show you the object you call for:

- Find all the blue sneakers.
- Find a red shirt.
- Find a freckle on yourself.
- Find a curly-haired girl or boy.
- Find a button on a dress.
- Find your own ankle.
- Find a pair of blue eyes.
- Find a shirt with stripes.
- Find all the white socks.

If you are playing with just one or two children, call out items that you see in the room around you.

Lens Games

Place objects under a magnifying glass and show the children how large and detailed an object becomes. Outdoors, experiment with binoculars, showing the children how to alternate the close-up and distant lenses. They can also look through cardboard cylinders from toilet paper or paper towel rolls; cover the end of the cylinder with colored cellophane and see how objects change color.

Perspectives

A child's awareness of his place in the world, and how it might be different, is the subject of these activities.

LOOKING UP AND ABOUT
Ask the children to lie flat on their backs, look up, and describe everything they see, as you prompt them. Then have the children turn over onto their tummies and look at the world from the perspective of the floor or ground. Do this both indoors and outside.

LOOKING DOWN
How powerful a child must feel when, used to looking up at adults all the time, she climbs up high and looks down at them instead. With your help and watchfulness, let the child sit on a ladder above you and look down. How funny to be taller! How funny to see the top of your head! Let the youngster look down at the objects in her own room and see them from a different perspective. If you are outdoors, children can get this exciting view from atop playground equipment.

CHAPTER FIVE

Magical Changes: Learning About Ourselves, Others, And Our World

ook at the little girl just given a new puppy: Her face lights up with a smile and her eyes dance. No words are necessary, for she has already told us how she feels better than words ever could. As adults, we know how to interpret gestures, the spring in a person's step, the droop in their shoulders, and of course, facial expressions. Such cues tell us a great deal about how people feel. But the ability to make sense of body language, natural as it may seem, is not something we are born with it. It is acquired in childhood.

Near the beginning of the 20th century, the famous psychologist and philosopher William James described the world of the newborn baby as "a blooming, buzzing confusion." It does seem likely that the world is a very confusing place for the baby, and that growing up is to a large extent a matter of learning to understand the

mysteries and the turmoil around us. To the baby and the young child, everything in the world appears to be constantly changing.

One especially volatile part of the child's world is the emotional behavior of people. Parents, other grown-ups, siblings, and other children all have abrupt mood swings. One moment Mommy is happy, the next she is annoyed. One moment Baby Brother is screaming and crying, and the next he is cooing with contentment. Even the child's own emotional swings can be puzzling. Learning about our mood swings and those of others is a complicated business that takes years. An important part of the process is learning how changes in mood are expressed through changes in a person's face.

The child's world seems unpredictable in countless other ways, too. Plants and children get taller; one friend moves away, then a new friend moves in; a building goes up where there used to be a field; Mommy and Daddy mix together rather dull ingredients, put them into an oven, and abracadabra! Out comes a cake! Over time, the young child learns that there is a reason or a logic behind the ever-changing physical environment.

The world also becomes less chaotic as the child learns that many events come in a predictable order. The sun rises and sets each day. The rain comes after the sky has clouded over, not before. The weather changes, but it rarely snows in July, and we seldom go swimming at the beach in January. The child learns, partly from stories and games, that each of the little stories of our lives—going shopping, taking a trip, eating a meal—has a beginning, a middle, and an end, and that this sequence is what makes the story work.

This chapter presents games designed to help children make sense of changes in mood, changes in size and shape, and changes in seasons and location. It is partly through playing games of this sort that children come to understand their world and themselves. §

EMOTIONAL AWARENESS AND SENSITIVITY

Young children are in the process of learning how feelings are conveyed by the body. That process is slow and sometimes difficult. It's not so hard for a child to learn that a smile signals that Mommy or Daddy is pleased, or that a scowl means something very different. But the next step—acquiring the sensitivity to other people's feelings that is the foundation of empathy—is trickier. Empathy is essential to healthy emotional development. By allowing us to experience things from another's point of view, it helps us to negotiate compromises, forgive others, share, and enjoy genuine caring. It is also instrumental in creative expression through poetry, stories, and plays.

Pretending games can help to further a child's emotional sensitivity considerably. Research has shown that training in make-believe play can make a big difference in developing children's awareness of other people's moods. The games described here provide the kinds of learning experiences children need to communicate in the mysterious, non-verbal language of emotion. As children master the games, they will increase their ability to empathize and become prepared for the more complex role-playing games that follow.

Making Faces

YOU WILL NEED:

- a mirror
- pictures depicting various emotions
- storybooks with pictures

Before children learn how to play roles, some practice in the imitation of emotions is helpful. In this game, children imitate the expression of several basic feelings: happiness, sadness, anger, surprise, and disgust. Begin by demonstrating an emotion through your own facial expression, and then ask the child to imitate the emotion you've expressed:

Watch me make a happy face.
(Smile broadly and crinkle your eyes.)
Can you make a happy face?
(Make a happy face.)

It's important to provide feedback about the child's efforts. You can do this by making an appropriate comment or by suggesting the required behavior:

See how my mouth turns down when I'm sad? Can you make your mouth turn down, like this? Oh, my! Now you look sad!

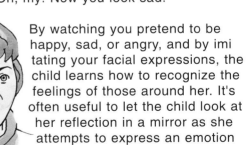

By watching you pretend to be happy, sad, or angry, and by imitating your facial expressions, the child learns how to recognize the feelings of those around her. It's often useful to let the child look at her reflection in a mirror as she attempts to express an emotion and compare her own expression with yours. You can also show her photographs or pictures from a magazine or read stories about children (see the appendix for suggestions), and ask the child to imitate the feelings experienced by the characters in the story.

Show Me

YOU WILL NEED:

- **a mirror**

You can make a game out of describing situations and asking the child to show you the feeling he would have in that situation:

Tell me, when would you make a happy face? Do you think you would be happy to hug a puppy? Show me your face.

Tell me, what kind of face would you make if your granddad came to visit and you didn't know he was coming? Show me a surprised face.

What kind of face do you have when it's raining outside and you can't go out to play? Show me a sad face.

Pretend that your best friend breaks your favorite toy and you are angry. Show me an angry face. Now make up with her and give her a hug. Show me a happy face.

Uh-oh. Your puppy accidentally went potty on the floor. Show me an "icky" face.

Use a mirror and let the children see their own expressions as they imitate each emotion. If a child has trouble expressing an emotion, demonstrate the appropriate expression and ask him to imitate your face. If you continue with vignettes like these, the children will become inventive and soon will tell you stories of their own and suggest the faces that go with them.

Let's Be Animals

YOU WILL NEED:

- **a story about animals**
- **pictures of animals**

Set the stage for the game by reading aloud a story about animals in the wild, at the zoo, or on a farm. At the same time, you might display pictures of the animals, which could be photographs, posters, images that the children cut from magazines, or even pictures that they draw. Following this introductory play, suggest that the children imitate the movements of the different animals.

horse—*gallop*
cat—*walk gracefully, leap, and climb*
kangaroo—*jump*
snake—*crawl along the ground*
monkey—*swing arms from tree to tree, scratch all over*
elephant—*swing arms in front for a trunk*
fish—*swim on the floor, jump for a fly*
bird—*arms out in flight*
mice—*walk with small, quick steps*
lion—*stalk about and roar*
seal—*flap arms like flippers*
caterpillar—*inch along the ground*

Start by suggesting that the child or children behave like one of the animals, such as a horse:

Let's pretend to be horses. What kind of sounds do horses make? They whinny, don't they, like this. *(Make a whinnying sound.)* And they gallop across the fields. *(Skip around to illustrate galloping.)* Can you whinny and gallop? Then you can become a horse! Become a horse and whinny and gallop across a field.

Now add a scenario for the children to play out. For example, tell them that a storm is coming across the field.

The horse sees the storm coming. What does he do? How does he sound now? *(Whinny in an urgent voice.)* What does he want to do? He wants to gallop back to the barn! *(Gallop to a spot under a large table or inside a circle of chairs.)*

Pretend to be other animals, such as lions who are hungry, cats who are determined to find mice, mice who don't want to be found, monkeys who love to play together, and so on.

Basket of Hats

YOU WILL NEED:

- **large basket or plastic laundry basket**
- **as many different kinds of hats as you can find**

Put a large assortment of hats, each associated with a different kind of activity, into a big basket. There should be hats like those worn by nurses, baseball players, police officers, fire fighters, train conductors, cowpokes, sailors, house painters, farmers, gardeners, and so on. Now let each child in turn choose a hat to wear. When they put on the hat, help them act out the character.

The wearing of a hat seems to change a child into another person. When Cowboy Joe is wearing his cowboy hat, there's no use calling him by his real name—he won't answer! These exercises will help children role-play characters and get the feel of being someone else.

BASEBALL HAT

Say, "Here's our amazing hitter. See her bat. Watch me throw the baseball." Pretend to throw a ball and call out, "Strike one! Strike two!" With the third pitch the child "hits" the ball; make believe it flies high. Encourage the other children to cheer and to follow the imaginary ball with their eyes while the hitter runs the bases for a home run.

GARDENING HAT

The child can fill a make-believe watering can, sprinkle imaginary flowers, pick some, smell them, arrange them in a beautiful bouquet, and give them to a friend.

NURSE'S HAT

Make believe one of the children is ill. Ask another child, the nurse, to look at the ill child's tongue, feel his forehead, take his pulse, and advise, "Drink lots of water, get some sleep, and call me back if you don't feel better soon."

FIRE FIGHTER'S HAT

Say, "Put on the hat. We all smell smoke. Pull the fire alarm! Here comes the fire engine." *(Make loud siren noises.)* "Firefighter, get your hose, the house is burning down. Save the family, everybody outside! Spray the water! Hooray, hooray, the fire is out!"

SAILOR HAT:

"The sailor is on his ship. The waves make the ship roll like this." *(Move from side to side.)* "The sailor sees a whale. He sees another ship. He looks through his spyglass." *(Cup hands, one in front of the other.)* "He sees some land. Land ho! Drop anchor and walk down the gangplank to shore. Back on land again."

MOMMY'S HAT

"It's morning. Mommy wakes up, gets dressed, eats breakfast, puts on the hat and says goodbye. She gets in the car and goes to work." The child sits on a chair or cushion and makes believe she is driving to work. Ask the children to point out familiar sights passed along the way. You may get them started by leading the way: "What does Mommy see on the way to work? Oh, look! There's a school. See the children playing outside? And there is a church; do you hear the bell ringing? And what's that up ahead? Do you see it? What is it?" Play this with Daddy's hat too.

This game provides an especially good opportunity to show that boys and girls can both participate in many of the same occupations: Girls can be fire fighters; boys can be nurses.

TRANSFORMATIONS

Children are fascinated by size and shape, and can often have strange ideas about these concepts. For example, they might think that shorter adults are younger than taller adults, or that people never stop growing. And if you have ever watched preschoolers try to carry a wide object through a door, you know that they often go at it with the object held horizontally, as though acting out an old Laurel and Hardy routine. When children play games involving size and shape, they begin to understand these concepts better.

Small Like a Ball, Big Like a Giant

This game teaches children to think about relative size by asking them to imagine changing their own size. Suggest that the children make themselves very small, like a ball, and then very large, like a giant. If they haven't any idea how to do this, demonstrate, first by bending your knees and head and wrapping your arms around your legs, and describe your movement:

Become a ball. Make yourself tiny and rolled up tight. Roll on the floor, little ball, be very small. Now become a giant! Grow tall like a giant. Taller, taller, stretch way up and walk around with big, big steps. Make believe you're a great big giant. Take BIG steps.

Playing music with this game increases the fun. You and the children can chant if you have no music recordings available:

Small like a ball, small like a ball, small like a ball... (spoken softly)
B-I-G like a giant! (spoken more loudly, and repeated as you begin to stretch up)

Ask the children to turn themselves into other small and big things:

Small like a pebble...big like a mountain!
Small like an apple...big like a tree!

Balloon

Have each child choose a partner (or be the child's partner yourself), and then ask one child to sit curled up on the floor like a balloon without any air in it while the other blows on his back, as though blowing up a balloon. Ask the "balloon" to pretend to get bigger and bigger, slowly extending his arms and puffing out his cheeks, and then, fully inflated, to float around the room. Now announce that all of a sudden the air has escaped from the balloon, and the balloon falls flat on the floor. Have the children take turns at being blower and balloon.

Change Your Shape

YOU WILL NEED:

• **old single or twin-size bed sheet**

This exercise asks children to change shape. Cut a pair of eye holes in a sheet so the children will be able to see, then demonstrate the game. Say, "When I'm covered with this magic sheet, I can take many different shapes. Watch!" Now drape the sheet over yourself so that you can see through the eye holes, and then take different shapes. You might begin by sitting on the floor with legs crossed and arms by your side and announce, "I'm a mountain, covered in snow." Then go on all fours and move about saying, "Now I'm a white elephant."

After a few such demonstrations of changing shape, invite your child to wear the sheet and take different forms by shifting her hands, legs, head, and torso. Encourage her to say what form she's taking and ask other children who are playing to imagine the object named. Say things such as, "Where's the tiger's head?" "Can you see the roof of the house?"

Magician

YOU WILL NEED:

• **long cape made of black fabric, such as crepe or rayon**
• **large safety pin or fastening tape**
• **"wand" (such as a chopstick)**
• **play dough or non-toxic soft modeling clay**

First demonstrate how the game is played. Put on the cape (best to use fastening tape), take a small piece of clay, roll it into a ball, and say:

When I wear this cape, I become a magician, and I can change one thing into another. This is an apple. Do you think I can change it into a banana? Just close your eyes and say the magic words, "Abracadabra, one, two, three."

Count slowly together, and while the children have their eyes closed, quickly roll the clay into a banana shape. Then announce, "Open your eyes! Here's the banana!" Let the children take turns wearing the magic cape, and put the play dough through other transformations, such as:

> ball into snake
> banana into tree
> ring into orange
> leaf into flower
> baseball bat into dog

You may need to help the magicians shape the clay. Don't worry about the realism of the object; it will look real enough to the children.

DEVELOPING SEQUENCE

Flowers bloom, and birds start building nests after all of the snow melts. Mom and Dad and older brothers and sisters usually stay home from work and school each time the days called Saturday and Sunday come around. Before serving tea to a guest, we first boil the water and let the tea steep.

Playing games is one way children learn that events often follow a particular order. Before a child serves make-believe tea to his teddy bear, for example, he goes through the pretend actions of putting the kettle on to boil, setting the table, placing a tea bag into a cup, and pouring the water into the cup. The game itself dictates the necessary sequence of events that lead to a satisfying play experience.

Four Seasons

YOU WILL NEED:

- **white sheet and green sheet**
- **artificial flowers, or pictures of flowers**
- **red, yellow, orange, and brown construction paper**
- **small brooms**

Spring, summer, fall, winter. Teach the children the words for the seasons that make a year, and have them repeat the sequence several times: spring, summer, fall, winter, spring summer, fall, winter.... The following game will help children learn the names and characteristics of the seasons as well as the idea that seasons follow one another in a regular sequence. Take each season in turn, beginning with the current one. Describe the characteristic weather of each season in your area, and then ask the children to pretend doing things appropriate for the season. A sample sequence is presented here:

SPRING

Spread a green sheet on the floor, and have on hand artificial flowers. Additional props are not necessary; you and the children can make believe you are holding a watering can and putting on your raincoat. Describe a spring scene such as the following, and act it out as you talk.

It's spring! Here's the new green grass that has just come up. Some days are chilly, and it rains a lot, but it's getting warmer. Birds are singing, and everywhere we see new plants emerging from the ground. *(Sprinkle artificial flowers on the sheet.)* Look at the pretty flowers that have just come up!

Spring is the time of year to plant a garden. Pretend you are a vegetable gardener. First we dig a row of little holes. Then we place seeds in the holes and cover them with dirt. Then we use our watering can to water the garden. Now watch the vegetables grow! What vegetables do you see?

Listen! A bird is singing in the tree. Pretend we are birds. Let's fly and build a new nest in the tree.

Let's smell all the flowers that are blooming. Mmmm!

Suddenly it starts to rain! Put on your raincoat and boots, and get your umbrella. Let's splash in the puddles! Catch rain in your pail. Take off your coat and get all wet!

Oh, look at all the mud that we got all over our shoes! Show me an icky face.

SUMMER

Tape a large yellow sun cut out of construction paper to the wall, leave the green sheet on the ground, and continue the pretend play:

> Spring has ended and now it's summer! The sky is blue, the sun is shining brightly, and it's hot outside. Put on your bathing suit, we are going to the beach. Spread out your towel on the sand, and grab your beach chair. Take your shovel and pail, and make a sand castle.

> Now pretend you go near the water. Let the water tickle your toes. Are you happy? Show me a happy face. Dry yourself off with a towel.

> Let's look for seashells. Pick up the shells that we see near the ocean. Do you see these colors: red, yellow, green, purple, pink? Count the shells.

FALL

Cut out leaves from red, orange, yellow, and brown construction paper, and if you like, have on hand play brooms or other items that can be used for "raking." Take down the large hot sun and push aside the green sheet as you introduce fall:

> Summer is over and now it's fall. The weather has turned chilly, so we have to put on our jackets. And the leaves are changing color, from green to yellow and red and brown. *(Hold up leaves of various colors cut from construction paper.)* In fall, the leaves fall from the trees. *(Drop the leaves.)*

> Let's pretend to rake leaves into a big pile. Name the colors of the leaves: red, yellow, orange, brown. Run, run, run, and jump into the big pile of leaves! What sound do the leaves make when you jump on them? Crunch. Crunch. Can you make that sound?

> It's a windy day. You are a leaf. You don't like to be stepped on. Show me an angry face! Now the wind comes along and lifts you right up into the sky. You are floating up in the sky. Now you are floating down. Let's all count to ten as you come floating down. 1, 2, 3, 4, 5, 6, 7, 8, 9, 10! You land on the pile of leaves. You feel happy. Show me a happy face.

WINTER

Spread a white sheet on the floor as you begin describing winter:

> The season has changed again. Now it's winter! And there's snow on the ground. The sky is gray and it's so cold!

> Oh no, your kitty has run away. You are sad. Show me a sad face. Let's find your lost kitty. It's cold outside. Pretend to put on your winter coat, hat, boots, and mittens to keep warm. You shiver. Your teeth chatter. Pretend to walk on soft, fluffy snow. Pretend to throw snowballs and to build a snow fort. Let's look for your kitty behind the snowman, in the woods, and in the snow fort. There she is! She is keeping warm in the snow fort. Pick up your kitty, hug her, and take her home. Show me a happy face.

> Now let's make snowmen. Now we'll make snow angels. Now get your shovel and shovel the sidewalk. Now let's go inside and get warm!

Airplanes in Flight

YOU WILL NEED:

- cushions, chairs, or boxes
- hats appropriate for a pilot and flight attendant
- serving trays
- assorted colorful lightweight scarves

AIRPLANE TRIP

Begin by discussing with the children the sequence of events involved in taking a plane trip: buying a ticket, checking the luggage, boarding the plane, fastening seat belts, taking off, landing, and deboarding. Then suggest they pretend to take a trip:

Let's take a pretend plane ride. First you must buy tickets. Everybody line up to buy your tickets! *(Hand each child an imaginary ticket.)*

Now you must check your luggage so that it can be put on the plane. Your luggage is heavy! Can you lift it? That's it, carry your luggage over here, and I'll see that it gets on the plane. Good.

Next we can get on the plane. Here is the plane. *(Arrange chairs, cushions, or boxes in a row.)* You are the pilot, Drew, so you sit up front. Nate and Susannah, you are flight attendants; you must see that everyone is seated and that their seat belt is on tight.

Is everyone ready for take-off? All right, Pilot, let's fly!

The children make believe the airplane is in flight, and that they can fly

anywhere in the world. They might go to the zoo and imitate the animals they see there. Or they might fly to Alaska, where they are cold and shiver and shake. Other fun places to land are a toy factory, a jungle, a farm, or a circus. The important part of this game is not the destination but the sequence of events that gets them to their destination.

BE AN AIRPLANE!

It's fun for the children to pretend that they are airplanes themselves. Have a collection of different colored scarves of a billowy fabric such as chiffon on hand. Let each child choose a colored scarf, hold it by a corner, and then sit on the floor in a circle. Say to the children:

> We are going to make believe we are airplanes. We can fly anywhere in the world. It's time to take off and fly! *(Get up and move around the room.)* Wave your scarf! You can go fast or slow, up or down. When I call out your color, come in for a landing.

This game is fun outdoors, where there is more space for moving freely, and the wind can pick up the scarves and billow them out. Encourage the children to improvise their movements and make sounds like jet engines.

CHAPTER SIX

Poems, Songs, and Stories: Paving the Way to Creative Expression

Rrrrr," says Andrew, "I'm driving my big truck to the store. I am bringing cookies and grapes and macaroni and cheese to the store, and then kids will have stuff to eat!" "I have lots and lots of dirt in my dump truck," says Chloe. "I am going to dump all the dirt in the driveway so the lady at this house can make a big garden." Three-year-old Chloe and Andrew are playing side by side in a sandbox, embellishing their games with descriptions of their fantasies, much as a musical score adds to our enjoyment of a movie. Beyond experiencing the sheer pleasure that comes from telling the stories they enact, children who use sounds and words as they play also improve their ability to express themselves.

Of course, what youngsters say aloud doesn't always come out quite right from an adult's point of view. James pretended to drive

around in a truck selling ice cream. He told us he was playing "college" and explained, "Daddy said he was an ice cream man when he was in college." Four-year-old Maria lined up all her toy soldiers "to rescue daddy" after hearing her mother say that her father was "tied up at work." As adults chuckle at the child's efforts to use new words and phrases, they do well to correct mistakes gently. Practice at using new words is essential for language development, and the mistakes that we find so amusing are an inevitable part of the child's learning process that we want to encourage.

Make-believe play gives the child a chance to try out overheard phrases and to connect or reshape them to fit the game. Often, playing with other children exposes a child to new word combinations and expressions. Shared make-believe games can therefore be very helpful in developing vocabulary.

When children play together they also suggest new roles to each other. Listen to groups of youngsters playing, and you will hear such things as:

"Make believe you're the mommy, I'm the daddy, and you're the baby."

"Make believe I'm the princess and you're the prince, and she can be the bad witch!"

"Let's play train. You be the conductor. You know, the one who takes the tickets."

ENCOURAGING CREATIVE EXPRESSION

Some children have a keen ability to take roles and enter into make-believe play without difficulty. Others are more self-conscious. They hang back, play more passively, or accept the roles thrust on them by their more outspoken playmates. But many children who play quietly by themselves or watch others in pretend play have the same capacity for make-believe as their more gregarious playmates. They just need a little help developing the content for their games, or the courage to try things on their own. Rather than leaving them to their own devices, parents and teachers should make a point of assuring these quieter children that pretending is a fine thing to do, and help them get started by offering suggestions and encouragement.

For example, Lianne rarely participated in the puppet, magic, or animal games we played with a group of four-year-olds. Instead, she played alone with plastic models or jigsaw puzzles, or followed the lead of a playmate who was riding a bike, skipping, or piling blocks up neatly. But after two weeks in adult-led pretend play, Lianne's hidden ability to make believe was blossoming. On one occasion, she sat at a bare picnic table with three little boys. "All right," she told the boys, "eat your dinner. Everybody eat up. Here's food for you, food for you, and food for doggy." (She leaned down and gave an imaginary dog imaginary food.) She was playing "mother," and these were her children, her pet, and her kitchen, complete with food and dishes. After the meal, she led the boys—and the dog—across the lawn to a little hill that she called the living room, and invited her family to "read and watch TV."

From then on Lianne's play was inventive, spontaneous, and filled with imaginary characters and objects. The shy little girl had been replaced by a child who sought out playmates, dealt deftly with an imaginary world, and took and assigned roles with ease. In the bargain, she was enriching her vocabulary and imagery, and developing self-assertiveness. Clearly, Lianne had always had the capacity for make-believe; all she needed was a little push.

Poems, songs, and stories are tools for helping children become more imaginative and creative. They provide a structure that children can follow easily, thus holding their attention, yet they stimulate thought that goes beyond the structure. Discussing the themes of poems, songs, and stories, for example, or asking children to create new characters or endings may stimulate imaginative thinking. As children become familiar with a poem, song, or story, they use the words they've heard and the roles they've played in new settings of their own invention, developing their innate gifts of creativity. §

POEMS

The activities in this section attempt to open the door to make-believe through poems, which can be thought of as structured word games. We favor the children's classics because their simple meter and rhyme make them easier for children to follow. It is also easier for children to remember the words of these poems, and to recite them with you. Ultimately, then, children are likely to use words and phrases from the poems in their own play. A good poem can therefore be a catalyst for imaginative play.

Poetry in Motion

This exercise asks children to put poems into motion—that is, act them out.

LITTLE JACK HORNER

Begin with this simple nursery rhyme that children know well:

> Little Jack Horner
> Sat in a corner
> Eating his Christmas pie.
> He put in his thumb
> And pulled out a plum
> And said, What a good boy am I!

As you recite the rhyme, act out the words. Sit in a corner, and pretend to eat a delicious pie with gusto, putting imaginary pieces of pie into your mouth and licking your lips and rolling your eyes. Pretend to stick your thumb in the pie and pull out a plum. Show the plum to the children using your fingers to indicate how big it is, then pop it into your mouth and chew it with great pleasure. Look pleased with yourself as you say, "What a good boy am I!" Pat yourself on the head and clap to show how pleased you are with your imaginary accomplishment. Now ask the children to act it out as you recite the words. Sit with the children as you recite the rhyme, and prompt them to make the appropriate gestures by making them yourself.

LITTLE MISS MUFFET

"Little Miss Muffet" is a natural follow-up because many of the movements are the same.

> Little Miss Muffet sat on a tuffet,
> Eating her curds and whey.
> Along came a spider and sat down beside her,
> And frightened Miss Muffet away.

Play together with your children as you recite the rhyme. Take turns being the spider, and try out as many variations of crawling and scaring Miss Muffet away as you can think of. As the children repeat the rhyme out loud and act it out, they not only expand their make-believe abilities but also gain mastery over the fear they are expressing and perhaps are even experiencing.

LITTLE BOY BLUE

Repeat this general procedure with other simple rhymes, such as "Little Boy Blue."

> Little Boy Blue
> Come blow your horn

Cup your hands in front of your mouth and say, "Toot! Toot!" or make another horn sound so that the children see that the body and the voice can serve as dramatic tools.

> The sheep's in the meadow
> The cow's in the corn

Get down on all fours and imitate the sheep ("baa, baa") and cow ("moooooo!").

Where is the boy
Who looks after the sheep?

Look around the room—under the table, behind the door—as though searching for him.

He's under the haystack
Fast asleep!

Pretend to discover him, then pretend to be him by stretching out on the floor and snoring. This rhyme is especially fun for three or four children. Each can take turns being the boy and the animals, and everyone can engage in an elaborate search for the missing Little Boy Blue.

Poetry in the Making

In this exercise, the idea is to collaborate with children to compose original poems. Begin by discussing rhyme. Explain that rhyming words have similar sounds: *Rat, mat, cat, hat, bat,* and *sat* all rhyme. Point out that many poems use words that rhyme. Illustrate by reciting lines from poems the children know, emphasizing the rhyming words: Little Jack *Horner* sat in a *corner*; Little Miss *Muffet* sat on a *tuffet*. You can then demonstrate how to make a poem by using words that rhyme. Be sure to put special emphasis on the rhyming words:

I put some green *beans*
In the pocket of my *jeans*.

A little bird will *rest*
In his warm, dry *nest*.

Now ask the children to make up poems of their own using two rhyming words that you provide, such as *red* and *bed,* or *tree* and *flea*. (A rhyming dictionary may come in handy here.) Write down the poems they compose so that you will be able to read them back to the children later—they will want to hear them again.

With older children, you can ask them to talk about something they like, and then make up a poem about it. Good topics for poems are simple ideas such as favorite foods, animals, things they wish for, things that fly in the sky, people they love, or a trip they took. Get the process started by asking the children to say something about the topic, then help them come up with rhyming words related to that topic. For example, if a child mentions that his dog has fleas, ask for words that rhyme with *flea*. The children might suggest *bee, see, he, tea, key,* and *me*, among others. Jot these words down, and then ask the children what they can say about fleas that use one or two of these rhyming words. Read the list aloud to help them consider the words. A child might suggest something like:

One day a *flea*
Came by for *tea.*

If the resulting poem has some humor, as this one does, so much the better. Remember that it's more important to have fun with words than to produce good poetry. Whatever your children come up with, recite it to them, and then ask them to recite it back so that they can savor the words and their success.

Sometimes you may be able to get the children to enlarge upon a poem to six or eight lines, but two or three lines are enough to make a poem for a preschooler. Whatever the length, try to use rhyme whenever possible since this gives the words a structure and rhythm. Encourage the children to provide the lines, and use what the children say with minimum alteration.

Always write the poems down so that you will be able to repeat them later. You may want to write the poems into a little scrapbook and have the children illustrate them.

SONGS

Songs, like poems, use words to express ideas, feelings, and images, with the added bonus of music. Most children enjoy singing as much as or more than reciting poems, and songs provide a great medium for group activities. Singing in the presence of others tends to help children feel more comfortable with others and may be especially "instrumental" in bringing out the shy child.

Music in Motion

YOU WILL NEED:

- tape or CD player
- music recordings

This exercise offers children the opportunity to move to the words in children's songs. In addition to helping them learn to follow simple instructions, such as hopping when the singer says, "Hop! hop! hop!," it gives them experience at moving about freely in front of others. With gentle encouragement, such activities can help make the shy child less inhibited.

Select recordings of songs that describe simple actions that children can perform, such as hopping, skipping, twisting, bending, and turning (see appendix for suggestions). Begin by playing at least part of the song and demonstrating the kind of actions to take and when to take them. With simple songs that describe a single action, you can embellish them in any number of ways, such as having the children clap with the rhythm or move in a circle.

You might also play lively songs that don't suggest specific movements, and encourage the children to skip, walk on tiptoe, sway, gyrate, wiggle, shake, bend, hop, turn, and move in other inventive ways to the rhythm. Playing music with different cadences and rhythms can help children better understand the connection between music and feelings, and learn to express a range of emotions.

Songs to Sing and Act Out

Many songs describe an activity that children can act out. For this exercise, choose songs that provide the opportunity for action and yet are familiar to the children or easy for them to learn. Songs that express concrete actions and repeat a simple refrain are best.

A good choice is, "Row, Row, Row Your Boat." The words are repetitive and enable the child to sit on the floor and imitate rowing movements vigorously without having to worry about intricate lines to sing.

Lay the groundwork for the activity by demonstrating how to row a boat. Sit facing the children so that they can see and imitate your actions. Announce that you are now going to sing a song about rowing a boat, and encourage the children to sing along with you. As you sing the words "row, row, row your boat, gently down the stream," rock back and forth, pretending to row, and encourage the children to row with you. As you sing "merrily, merrily, merrily, merrily," smile and toss your head from side to side with the rhythm of the words. Then while singing "life is but a dream," put your hands together and lay your head down on them as though sleeping. Finally, straighten up and row again as you begin another chorus of the song.

One fun variation is to sing and act out "Row, Row, Row Your Boat" in pairs. You and your child, or pairs of children, sing the song while sitting and facing each other, holding hands, and rocking to and fro in rhythm.

Sing and act out other songs such as "The Farmer in the Dell" and "Old MacDonald" in the same way. Exaggerating the motions adds humor and delight to the game, and also helps the child remember the song.

Musical Backgrounds

Just as moviemakers use musical soundtracks to enhance their stories on film, parents and teachers can play recorded music in the background while engaging in imaginative games with children. Music encourages emotional expression and suggests ideas for content for the children's games. Classical recordings and other instrumental music are well suited to the following games.

YOU WILL NEED:

- **tape or CD player**
- **music recordings**

SINGLE SCENES

Play music while acting out a single action or characteristic. For example, you might choose music that suggests any of the following:

soaring like a seagull

riding a horse

falling asleep

driving on a bumpy road

ballet dancing

conducting an orchestra

riding a bicycle down a hill

catching an ocean fish

FULL STORIES

Play music as a background for more elaborate scenarios, such as:

a visit to a haunted house, with green goblins mixing a mysterious brew, witches flying on broomsticks, and black cats scurrying across the room;

a space trip, with rocket ships taking off and landing on moons and planets, and astronauts moving slowly as if they have no weight and discovering odd objects and strange creatures;

an ocean voyage, with children imitating the noises of the wind, the movement of the waves, the rocking of a buoy, and the sound of a ship's horn, then landing on an island and exploring it, digging for treasure, building a lean-to, looking for food, fishing in the ocean, cooking their catch, and imitating noises of strange birds and animals.

Start the music and describe the situation, using your voice expressively to echo the tone of the music, whether it is soothing or agitated, happy or melancholy, stormy or quiet. Let the children take over as much as possible as they act out the experience to the music.

STORIES

Acting out stories is a great way to develop both the imagination and social skills. The child who plays a part in a story acquires a much more intimate understanding of the story than one who merely listens to it. The child comes to understand not only that story better, but also the structure and functions of stories in general. Performing stories is also good preparation for the sociodramatic play described in the next chapter. You can get some story ideas from the appendix.

Familiar Favorites

Start with simple stories that the children are already likely to know, because a familiar tale is easier for the child playing a role for the first time. Also, children are less self-conscious if the story is already part of their world. Read the story aloud several times, over the course of several days, before asking the children to act it out.

"Goldilocks and the Three Bears" is a good choice. We prefer the version in which Goldilocks is invited to stay for dinner rather than being chased away, but you may want to try them both. Proceed by telling the story and directing the children at the same time:

> Once upon a time, there were three bears. Would someone like to be one of the bears? Oh, good! Ted, you be Papa Bear; Mattie, you can be Mama Bear; Philip, you can be Baby Bear.

Continue with the story, describing the preparation of the porridge and sitting down to eat it:

> Papa Bear tries the porridge and he says….

Give Papa Bear a chance to say, "This porridge is too hot!" If he doesn't, say the line for him in a deep, bear-like voice, and then ask him to repeat it. Next turn toward Mama Bear and say,

> Mama Bear tries the porridge and she says….

Now wait for Mama Bear to say her line, and proceed as before. Continue in this way to the end of the story, narrating and helping Goldilocks and the bears say their lines and act out their parts. When you reach the end, be sure to applaud the performance and cry "Bravo!"

When the children have acted out the story once, they may want to repeat it immediately. If you have more children than roles, give children who have not participated the chance to play. Each time the children dramatize the story, encourage them to take on more and more of their role, saying their lines with feeling and appropriate facial expressions and embellishing the action—entering the house, tasting the porridge, finding Goldilocks—with details. Eventually the children may spontaneously act out the entire story while you provide only the barest narrative.

Expanding the Repertoire

Once they begin playacting, the children will want to perform many more of their favorite stories. With practice in playacting familiar plots, they will soon want to act out their own made-up tales, or recent events in their lives, such as:

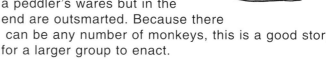

> a birthday party
> a picnic
> a bus trip
> a visit from Grandma
> a visit to the firehouse
> getting a haircut
> a trip to the aquarium

You may also acquaint them with other, less familiar storybooks that lend themselves especially well to playacting. One of our favorites is *Caps for Sale*, written and illustrated by Esphyr Slobodkina (see the appendix), in which mischievous monkeys steal a peddler's wares but in the end are outsmarted. Because there can be any number of monkeys, this is a good story for a larger group to enact.

Puppet Show

YOU WILL NEED:

- **puppet theater**
- **puppets**
- **chairs or floor cushions**
- **construction paper**

Construct a puppet theater that enables young puppeteers to sit on the floor behind some sort of screen and not be seen. A large appliance box with a cutout stage, such as the one pictured here, makes a beautiful theater, as does a large piece of cardboard that is supported on either side. If you wish, decorate the puppet theater, and hang a small curtain from a dowel or rod at the front of the box. Thrust the dowel through the sides of the box near the top. The children can easily separate the curtain and move each half aside before the show begins. You can purchase ready-made puppet theaters, but building them is at least half the fun.

Place chairs or cushions in front of the puppet stage for the audience. Create a theater atmosphere by having your children make play money and tick-ets from construction paper. They can even prepare a simple illustrated program. Music can be furnished by children playing the kinds of instru-ments described in "Do-It-Yourself Band" on page 71. These preparatory activities allow everyone to get involved and perform a role of sorts: Those who are not puppeteers are ticket sellers, ticket collec-tors, program distributors, or musicians.

Fashion puppets from paper bags, old socks, mit-tens, or old rubber balls placed on sticks. Use scraps of fabric, ribbon, yarn, and other notions to decorate them, or draw features on with paint or markers. You can also buy puppets, of course, but again, children enjoy making them, and doing so is a fine activity for a rainy day.

The kinds of stories described earlier in this sec-tion can be acted out with the puppets. Once you get them started, children are likely to invent their own plots, and at each show they will enlarge and change the story line. Some children are more comfortable acting out a story through pup-pets than they are performing a role themselves. During a puppet show, you have only to provide the same sort of prompting of lines and actions suggest-ed earlier. And always applaud and shout "Bravo!" at the end of a performance, and encourage the audience to do so as well.

CHAPTER SEVEN

Roles to Play By: The Butcher, the Baker, the Candlestick Maker

Five-year-old George is playing "going to work" at his nursery school. He makes and eats breakfast, washes the dishes, and then dons a man's hat and a woman's pocketbook. He gets into the family car—a plastic cube turned upside down—and drives off to the office with lots of noisy imitations of horns blowing, motors rumbling, and bye-bye waves. George is imitating both his mommy and his daddy in their daily routine, and he is also doing much more. George is learning about social roles.

In every society that anthropologists, psychologists, and sociologists have studied, there are clearly defined roles that its members are expected to play. Some roles are more appropriate for certain ages than others; some are assigned more to one sex than the other; some involve work whereas others involve recreation; some focus on

material things, others are more spiritual. Pretend play is one of the best ways children can learn about the roles people play in society.

Through pretend play, preschoolers explore grown-up roles that include not only mommy and daddy, but also schoolteacher, doctor, nurse, police officer, fire fighter, letter carrier, athlete—the butcher, the baker, the candlestick maker. Through stories and television, they also learn about soldiers, explorers, astronauts, kings, queens, angels, spies, fairies, and supernatural figures. Each of these roles has defining characteristics: many roles such as nurse, police officer, and athlete involve special costumes; astronauts, soldiers, and other roles use distinctive vocabulary or equipment; and some roles have strictly defined rules or conventions associated with them.

As a parent or teacher, you play a critical part in helping the child identify and understand the array of roles in our culture. Children observe your behavior as mommy, daddy, or teacher, and they notice the way you respond to the store keeper, the principal, other parents—learning from you the importance and the acceptability of these roles. During make-believe play with your children, the roles you assign and take on yourself are also important. Helping your children role-play in make-believe games prepares them for the actual social roles that await them.

THE BENEFITS OF ROLE-PLAYING GAMES

A fundamental aspect of a person's identity is captured by the terms male and female. Today we are in the midst of a transition in Western society, as sex roles are changing and overlapping. Boys and men increasingly perform tasks previously considered female, while girls and women increasingly do things formerly considered suitable only for their male counterparts. Girls and boys who cook and sew and wash dishes during pretend play, and who then pretend to be doctors and fire fighters, astronauts and mountain climbers, are preparing for the widest range of roles available to them in the future.

Role playing also teaches children all sorts of facts about their world. A game of "going to the supermarket" helps them learn about concepts such as color, size, weight, and cost. It also teaches them that clothes and food and the other items we use do not appear magically out of thin air. And as they move through the aisles, choose items, read prices, pay at the checkout, bring their items home, and prepare meals, they learn sequence and structure, which is the foundation for planful thinking. In the short term, these structured games also prepare the child for the formal arrangements of school.

Another benefit of role-playing games is that they help teach children how to behave and what to expect in a variety of situations. Indeed, the child who has played "school" is better prepared, when the time comes, for the challenges that actual school entails. The child who has played "doctor" is not so frightened by the pediatrician's touch or the feel of a cold stethoscope. Children who have embarked upon pretend camping trips in their backyard or on the playground have a better idea of what to expect in the woods.

Role-playing games require a spontaneity and a give-and-take that help the child learn to deal effectively with other people. When you encourage your child to play these games, you open the door to many new ways of making contact with other children and learning further roles along the way. One of the most constructive features of nursery school and of free play in backyards and playgrounds is children's interaction around pretend games. The child who grasps the terms of "space trip" or "picnic" moves smoothly into a small group. As the children assign each other roles and take turns at them, they not only discover new roles but also learn to accommodate to the demands of the game or to the mood of the group, developing their skills of flexibility and problem solving.

Equally important, they learn to look at situations from different points of view, for sometimes they are the "bad guys," and sometimes they are "victims." Research has shown that children who have learned to see another child's point of view through role playing are much less likely to become physically aggressive. Our own experience has shown us that such play often improves social relationships.

IDENTIFYING PROBLEMS THROUGH ROLE-PLAYING

Sometimes role-playing games provide insight into problems that a child is having. A boy who has been poorly prepared for school, for example, may reveal this through a game in which school and jail get mixed up. Or a girl who is very jealous of a new baby in the family may play games in which an imaginary crying baby or a doll is scolded or spanked or subjected to horrendous punishments. Such games can sometimes help to solve the very problems they bring to light. For the child who confuses school with jail, a pretend game that emphasizes the more pleasant aspects of school—such activities as finger painting, storytelling, and lunchtime—can lead him to look forward to the experience. For the child who resents a new baby, a game in which she learns about the enhanced status of being a big sister can provide an entirely new view of the previously unwelcome intruder. By paying more attention to her and introducing themes of caretaking and sharing into make-believe games of "big sister," you can help the child gain a sense of self-esteem and handle her anger and jealousy in a more constructive fashion.

HOW GROWN-UPS CAN HELP

To get the most benefit out of these games, children need the help of adults who know when to fade into the background. The adult's job is to suggest a game, help set the scene by providing simple costumes and props, and get the dialogue rolling—and then let the children take over. Adults who persist in helping by suggesting lines and correcting errors often reduce, rather than increase, the value of the game. It doesn't matter if the events are out of sequence or if the facts are inaccurate. You need to be there when help is requested, or to settle a disagreement that threatens to spoil the game. But otherwise, let the children make believe in their own way with their own materials and ideas.

The games in this chapter are presented in three categories. Neighborhood games involve ordinary roles performed by people in the community: store clerks, waiters, teachers. We also describe games that are especially suited for children who must, for one reason or another, play without other children. And finally, we discuss games of high adventure that give children a chance to push their imaginations to the limit. Most of these games will appeal more to four- and five-year-olds than to younger children, but the ability and willingness of children to participate varies greatly, so don't automatically exclude the three-year-old. Finally, these games are merely samples of the kinds of activities that adults can suggest to get children started in role-playing, and should be viewed as springboards. Once initiated, children will often invent their own roles and games—and their own special worlds. §

NEIGHBORHOOD GAMES

Children love to learn about the people and places in their community. Routine experiences at the store, the post office, the restaurant, and the library are treasure troves of learning for the preschooler. In addition, there are many places that people visit less routinely but are equally vital or fascinating, such as the firehouse, the zoo, or the police station.

As part of your preparation for neighborhood games, arrange visits or field trips to a restaurant, the post office, and other community places, so that the children can actually see adults doing the things they will later imitate. Parents should consider taking their child with them as much as possible on errands, for the same reason.

When you play these games, start by talking with your children about the experiences they've had. Describe or remind them of the people and the sequence of events involved in going to a restaurant, mailing a letter at the post office, checking out a library book, or purchasing groceries. Ask them what they recall about the roles they have seen on their excursions—what sorts of things the car wash attendant, the postal clerk, and the waiter said and did. What did the fire fighter, the police officer, and the grocery clerk wear? What things did the librarian and the zoo keeper use or work with? Based on their answers and your prompting, help your children find or make costumes and props that will bring the games to life.

School

YOU WILL NEED:

- tables and chairs
- school supplies
  (e.g., paper, markers, crayons)
- schoolroom props
  (e.g., chalkboard, clock, posters of numbers and the alphabet, bell, easel)
- gold stars or other stickers for rewards

Introduce the children to the game by describing in sequence a typical school day and some of the things that "big boys and girls" do at school:

writing their names or the ABCs, counting to 10, listening to stories, having show and tell, drawing pictures, eating in the cafeteria, and playing on the playground.

With this background, ring a bell or call out, "Time for school!" The children can take turns playing the roles of teacher and student. You might even include arriving by bus—complete with a child playing the role of bus driver—in the game. Let the children direct the game as much as possible, but if the child who plays teacher needs a little help, quietly suggest an activity. Teacher might lead the other children in a game of "Simon Says," or have them sing a song, draw pictures, or write their name or any other assignment. It doesn't matter whether the children are able to print letters and numbers yet; pretending while scribbling is just as much fun as the real thing. Teacher can put gold stars on the children's artwork and paperwork to show what a good job they've done. Then teacher can have all of the students line up and walk to the "cafeteria" for lunch, or outside for "recess."

House Painters

YOU WILL NEED:

- large box or large sheets of cardboard
- plastic containers for paint
- children's water–soluble paint
- inexpensive paintbrushes or foam trim bushes
- discarded shirts to serve as smocks
- lots of paper towels

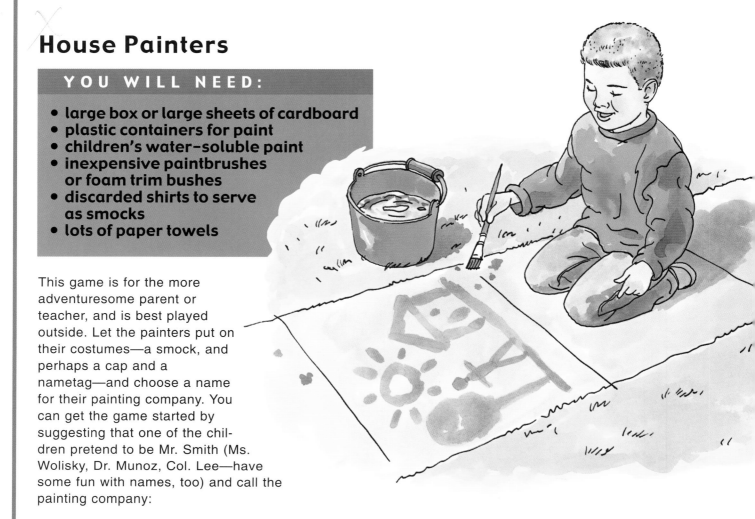

This game is for the more adventuresome parent or teacher, and is best played outside. Let the painters put on their costumes—a smock, and perhaps a cap and a nametag—and choose a name for their painting company. You can get the game started by suggesting that one of the children pretend to be Mr. Smith (Ms. Wolisky, Dr. Munoz, Col. Lee—have some fun with names, too) and call the painting company:

> Hello, is this the Wet Paint Company? This is Mr. Smith. The paint on my house is dirty and peeling off. Would you come over and paint it, please?

The painters will naturally respond enthusiastically, "We'll be right there!" Let the children make a paint catalog or paint chips so that the painters can show color choices to the customer. (This also provides a chance to practice color naming.) After the customer selects a color, the job begins. The child playing the customer can now switch roles and become one of the painters.

The "house" can be a large appliance box, or large pieces of cardboard propped up or taped together. Cut out or draw doors, windows, and shutters. Use water-soluble paint, such as finger paint or tempera diluted with water, or use water with food coloring, as the children are likely to go through lots of it. Let the children experiment with mixing the colors and with the strokes. This kind of play needs an adult close by to ensure that things don't get out of hand. Of course, some mess and minor skirmishes are to be expected, but the fun is worth it.

You can also play a simplified variation of "house painters" with a bucket of water, a brush, and a sidewalk. Your child can use the sidewalk as a canvas and "paint" pictures of houses with water. This is a good activity for younger preschoolers or when your child needs something to do for 30 minutes.

Shopping

YOU WILL NEED:

- boxes and/or tables for counters and shelves
- store products (e.g., harmless toiletries such as soap, food boxes, clothing, shoes, books, play hammers and garden equipment, bakery goods, depending on the type of store)
- play shopping bags
- cash box or toy cash register
- play money

Pretend shopping can take various forms, with children going to a grocery store, shoe store, hardware store, clothing store, or bookstore. The game can include shopping at several stores, one after the other, while the children variously play the roles of customer and salesperson.

Encourage the customers to look over the items and ask questions about them. In a grocery store they might ask: "Do you have any bananas today?" "Is this fish fresh?" "Where can I find the corn?" "How much is this bread?" Suggest dialogue that suits the store and product. If the setting is a shoe store, for example, you might suggest a dialogue something like this:

Customer: Hello. I need to buy a pair of shoes. Can you show me what you have?
Salesperson: Let me measure your foot.... You need size 3. What color shoe would you like?

Customer: Hmm. Those red ones look nice.
Salesperson: Here you are. Let's see if these fit.

If the shopping is to be at a bakery, then some baked goods are in order. Homemade cookies of various kinds are one obvious solution (if the sales staff don't eat up the entire inventory), but food made from play dough offers a fine substitute. The children can mold and "bake" the products and then offer them in the store.

Whatever the type of store, after examining the goods the customer makes a selection and enacts the process of paying the salesperson. This can consist of simply handing the salesperson some play money, or it can involve sale prices, making change, and receipts, depending on how old the children are and how elaborate they can make their play. Here is another good opportunity for children to practice their politeness skills.

Once you have demonstrated the general procedure for shopping in a given store, the children will usually take over. With several children, roles can include customer, salesperson, cashier, and even delivery person. Have them take turns playing who's who.

Library

YOU WILL NEED:

- children's books
- one or more tables
- cardboard boxes
- index cards

A visit to the local library before playing this game will help children understand this special place. Pay extra attention to the check-out desk and the card catalog or on-line catalog area.

Set up your library by arranging a selection of books on a table. Create a check-out desk and a desk with a "computer" (a cardboard box) used to locate cataloged books. Have the children make library cards for themselves by decorating index cards or pieces of cardboard on which you have printed their names.

Start the game by asking one or more children to be librarians while you take the part of a patron. Look over the selection of books, and ask if the library has any material on, say, dinosaurs. (Ask about something that is in plain view.) You might sit at the computer and search for information on the topic. ("I think I'll see if the computer can give me information on dinosaurs. Hmmm. Yes, that looks like a book I could use.") Select a book to borrow, and say to one of the librarians, "I'd like to take this. Here's my library card." If your local library still hand-stamps books, show the children how to stamp the book; if the library uses a computer system, show the children how to imitate the procedure. Ask when the book is due back. ("Is this book due back in two weeks?")

Rainy days are ideal for library play. As a special treat you can provide a story hour by letting each child choose a short story for you to read.

Encourage the children to take turns being librarians and patrons. In addition to selecting books to borrow, patrons can ask librarians for help in finding information on various topics. Librarians can help patrons find books and search for information on computers. Given some sheets of paper, they can even "print out" information from the computer and give it to a patron: "Here is the information you requested about dinosaurs."

Doctor

YOU WILL NEED:

- bandages
- old sheet cut up for slings
- adhesive tape
- toy stethoscope
- costume items (e.g., white shirts for the doctor and nurse)
- eye chart
- toy phone
- bathroom scale
- blanket or pad to lie on
- makeshift "instruments"
- pad of paper or notebook for doctor

Arrange a doctor's office that consists of an examination room and a reception area. One child can play the receptionist who talks to sick people on the phone and greets other children who play patients. Another child might play a nurse, who asks for the patient's name and escorts the patient to the examining room. Have a pad or blanket on the floor for the patient to lie on, with all the necessary materials arranged on a box, tray, or little table nearby: bandages, stethoscope, other instruments. Let the children use their imaginations with harmless kitchen utensils and other gadgets.

The doctor diagnoses different ailments: eye trouble (bring out the eye chart), broken arm (splint, bandages, and sling), sore throat (say "ahhh")—any disease or condition that occurs to him or her. The doctor might also conduct routine check-ups, measuring height, weight, pulse, and blood pressure, listening to the patient's breathing, and offering plenty of advice. The doctor records all findings on a pad of paper. Encourage the children, boys and girls alike, to take turns playing doctor, nurse, patient, and receptionist. With more children you can play "hospital," and include an ambulance driver.

You may need to help start the dialogue, but the children will soon take over. As you listen to what they say, expect to learn quite a bit about their thoughts, concerns, and amusing misconceptions about doctors, health, and their own bodies.

Car Wash

YOU WILL NEED:

- ride-on vehicles, tricycles, and wagons
- rags, sponges, and pails
- a garden hose, for extra fun

"Car wash" is a perfect game for a hot summer day, played outdoors with lots of water. While some children are the customers driving their vehicles into the car wash, others are the car washers. Everyone gets deliciously wet!

Customers line up in their ride-on cars, trucks, bikes, and trikes, and drive them into the car wash, which can be set up on a driveway, sidewalk, patio, or lawn. Washers fill their pails with water and wipe down the cars with rags and sponges; if you permit use of a hose, remove any nozzle so that the flow is gentle. The children can make a sign out of cardboard, which might list the name of the car wash and even the price for washing and waxing. If collecting money is part of the game, they can employ a box as a cash register and make play bills to exchange. Adults can help with the dialogue, which might go something like this:

Drive right up!
Close all the windows.
Leave the key in the car.
Do you want plain wash or wash with wax?

The children can switch roles freely, driving up to the car wash, and then becoming the car wash attendants who scrub down their own wheels.

An indoor version of "car wash" can be played using toy cars and trucks. The child can construct a car wash alley with blocks, and use a watering can for the rinse spray. If water is used, be sure to set up on a plastic sheet, or place a towel on a tile or concrete surface under the car wash.

Restaurant

YOU WILL NEED:

- **tables and chairs**
- **small notebook and pencil**
- **menus**
- **table settings**
- **tray**
- **finger food**
- **play money**

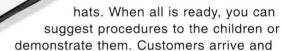

Start by setting up the restaurant, which can be indoors or out—a formal dining room, a casual bistro, or an outdoor café! Set the table or tables. Encourage the children to use their imaginations to come up with centerpieces, which might consist of real or artificial flowers, pictures of flowers cut out of magazines, a bowl of fruit, unlit candles or lanterns, or virtually any item or collection of items that is interesting or colorful. Try including paper place mats that the children decorate. Show the children where the napkin and each dish and piece of flatware goes, either paper or plastic or toy versions. Have a small notebook on hand to serve as an order pad for the waiter. Create menus; the children might make them by pasting pictures of food onto a sheet of construction paper.

Consider costumes to fit the roles: the waiter might wear an apron, and the customers might wear hats. When all is ready, you can suggest procedures to the children or demonstrate them. Customers arrive and hang up their coats, the waiter welcomes them, shows them to a table, and gives them a menu. After consulting the menu, the customers place their order, and perhaps the waiter recommends a favorite dish or two. As an extra treat, the children can serve and eat actual finger foods (e.g., raisins, cookies, crackers, cheese, and any other snacks that you have to offer) while pretending they are the delicacies from the menu. The food can arrive in courses: appetizer, salad, entrée, dessert, which the waiter presents with a flourish. Here is a chance for everyone to practice words such as "please," "thank you," and "you're welcome." Finally the waiter clears the table and presents the check. The happy diners tip generously!

Post Office

YOU WILL NEED:

- shoe boxes or similar cartons
- old envelopes
- stickers
- junk mail, old magazines, old postcards
- real or makeshift scale
- slotted cardboard box
- pretend mail sack (e.g., shopping bag, tote bag, backpack)
- maps, real or handmade

Set up a post office on a table. Place envelopes and "stamps" (stickers) on the table, and display a large slotted collection box for mailing letters. Line up open boxes (shoe boxes work especially well) on the table for sorting the junk mail, old magazines, and postcards, which will serve as the children's mail. Pin up local, state, or national maps.

A child playing the role of postal clerk stands behind the table, sells stamps, and sorts mail into the shoe boxes. Customers come to the post office to buy stamps and mail letters and packages. Parents and teachers can demonstrate buying a stamp, weighing a letter or package, placing stamps on the items, and dropping letters in the slot of the collection box to get the children started. Refer to the maps, and talk about how long it takes for a letter or package to be delivered, depending on how far it has to go.

Expand the game by including mail delivery. Close up the post office. Each child goes to a "house" (a sofa, a desk, a small corner of the room). The letter carrier places the sorted mail into a bag that serves as the mail sack and delivers the mail to each address. Everyone gets mail. Be sure each child gets a chance to play the postal clerk or the letter carrier.

SOLITARY GAMES

Sometimes a child has no available play-mates. Several of the preceding games can be adapted for a single child, but the games in this section are especially suited for these solitary occasions.

In the games described earlier, different children take the various roles: one child is a librarian while another is a library patron; one child is the doctor while another is the nurse and still another is the patient; and so on. When a child engages in pretend play on his own, he must either play all roles himself, switching from one character to another, or turn the other roles over to imaginary playmates or use stuffed animals.

Many adults worry about the effects of imaginary playmates on a child's mental health. They hear about people suffering from serious mental illness who hear and see things that aren't there, and they wonder if this might have started with imaginary playmates. We can assure parents and teachers that there is no evidence that imaginary companions in childhood are anything other than a perfectly normal form of make-believe.

In fact, as discussed in chapter 1, imaginary playmates can offer substantial benefits, especially to a child who is on his own much of the time. For example, sleeping alone at night can sometimes be frightening for the child between the ages of two and five. When the lights are off, the familiar environment becomes strange and mysterious. The play of light and shadow on the wall, and the noises from the house and the street, may conjure fears of danger lurking unseen. At such times, an imaginary friend who can "talk" to the child and share the danger is a great comfort.

For the games that follow, we recommend that you play with your child the first time through so that he knows the basics. Afterward, he can play by himself or with an imaginary friend, developing variations and details of his own.

Newspaper Reporter

YOU WILL NEED:

- **large sheets of blank paper**
- **pencils and markers**
- **photographs, or instant or disposable camera**
- **old magazines**
- **glue sticks**
- **newspapers**

This game is best suited for older preschoolers. Begin by showing the child an actual newspaper. Talk about the word "news," and why people want to know about it. Point out the different kinds of news a newspaper contains (e.g., events, weather, sports, advertisements, cartoons, letters to the editor, announcements), and the different kinds of events: local, national, and international; political, social, and scientific. Draw attention to the headlines and photographs that accompany each story.

Talk to your child about creating her own newspaper and the role of reporter. Have some fun coming up with a name for the paper. Print the name, or help the child print it, on top of several large sheets of blank paper, using a heavy marker. Now discuss some of the kinds of news items the child might write about for a newspaper of her own: an accident (Daddy dropped a dish and it broke); how to feed goldfish; a problem (the family dog chews on the furniture, baby brother cries at night); the coming birthday of a relative; the arrival of a new neighbor; the cat that got stuck up a tree; a family yard sale.

Help your child write a story and paste it on the newspaper with a glue stick. Depending on her skill level, writing a story might mean scribbling, dictating a story that you transcribe, or writing a story for herself. Give the story a headline using a dark marker, and include the child's name, or "by-line." Your cub reporter can illustrate the story with drawings she makes, or she can search through magazines for pictures to paste next to the story or use extra family photos. She can even use an instant or disposable camera to take her own photographs. Take her with you to get the film developed.

Once the game is under way, let the child work on her own when she is able, but look in on her progress frequently and help her write stories, find illustrations, and do "paste up" to keep the game going. When the paper is completed, post it in a prominent place, such as a message board or the refrigerator door. Also, help your child make photocopies to distribute to family members, neighbors, and friends.

Camping Trip

YOU WILL NEED:

- **knapsack or backpack**
- **canteen or bottle with a twist off top**
- **sleeping bag or old pillowcase**
- **small tent**
- **play fishing pole**
- **play eating and cooking utensils**
- **flashlight**
- **snack food**

Your child can be a camper indoors or out. As a preliminary step, look at books and magazines that depict nature settings. When it is time to play, get your camper started on his trip by helping him pack the backpack and walking around the play area, pretending that you are looking for a quiet place in the woods near a make-believe river or stream:

Hmmm. How about this spot? There's a little stream here, a nice level area to sleep on, and the big trees provide lots of shade. Shall we camp right here?

When you've agreed on a good camping spot, set up a small tent (or a makeshift tent using a blanket) and a sleeping bag (or a pillowcase). Pretend to bait hooks and catch a fish or two from the stream. Dig a pit and circle it with rocks, then build a make-believe campfire in the circle, and cook the fish in a frying pan over the fire. (If the game happens to be played around the noon hour, you might make hot dogs and then return to the game, pretending the food has just been cooked in camp. Otherwise you can eat the snack food, pretending it is your fish.)

Sing some songs and roll into the sleeping bag for a snug night's sleep. Wake up suddenly and say, "What was that! I heard something moving through the trees." Shine the flashlight. "Look! It's only a deer, grazing on the grass." Go back to sleep and then awake again. It's morning and time to hike home. Make believe you are seeing wild animals and birds, trees and flowers, and different kinds of terrain.

Gardener

YOU WILL NEED:

- play garden tools
- watering can
- seed packets or bedding plants
- topsoil from a garden center
- artificial flowers

This game can take place in a real garden or a pretend garden. Before you begin the game, talk about the growth cycle of plants, and their need for good soil, water, and sunshine. Go outside and get an up-close look at good garden soil: its dark color, its earthy scent, its feeling of cool dampness, its crumbly texture. And as always, find suitable clothes, such as a floppy hat, gardening gloves, and a smock or overalls, to serve as a gardener's costume.

In the pretend garden, a rug can serve as the garden bed. First the child digs up the soil, using a plastic shovel, hoe, and cultivator, or other items that can serve as these tools. She then pretends to plant seeds, cover them with soil, water them, and watch them grow. If she is growing flowers, she can pretend to pick them, smell them, arrange them in a vase, and put them on display on a table. Use artificial flowers in the arrangements, or have fun by making flowers from construction paper and pipe cleaners or other materials. If her bounty consists of vegetables and fruits, she can place real apples, pears, corn, and other items in her garden bed to harvest, then carry them to the kitchen to prepare to eat.

The real garden can be a small plot or planter outside. Be sure to prepare the soil with your child; purchase a bag of topsoil from a garden store, and if possible add some compost or other organic matter such as leaf mold. Good soil will help ensure healthy plants, so your junior gardener won't be disappointed. You can start from seeds, or purchase bedding plants, or a combination of both. Annuals are a good choice, because most are fairly sturdy, and they grow and flower quickly. Check the plants daily. Water them (but don't drown them!), and watch them grow taller and finally bloom. Most children find this experience almost magical.

As an indoor alternative, your child can also suspend a carrot top or sweet potato over a water-filled container with toothpicks, so that the bottom of the plant is in the water. Place the dish in a sunny window, and check the water level every day. The vegetable will begin to grow and produce leaves quickly and easily.

The indoor pretend garden and the efforts with real plants can take place simultaneously. The child will learn to tend her real garden by working in the pretend version, and the delay of waiting to pick the real flower can be eased through the make-believe play.

Wildflower Seeds

Red Poppy

Papaver rhoeas

ADVENTURE GAMES

Children need to run and whoop and holler. This may be hard on adults, especially when it occurs indoors, but the pleasure youngsters get from a good adventure game—pirates, Robin Hood, wild west, submarines, spaceships, Vikings—is worth it. And they get more than mere entertainment.

Imagine how the world must appear to the preschool-age child: It is complex, mysterious, and at times frightening. Most of the people in it (parents, teachers, older siblings) are much bigger and are constantly controlling the younger child's behavior. Dressing up and becoming a hero allows a child to feel important, powerful, and independent, if only for the moment. Children want to master the numerous physical and psychological challenges they encounter every day, but often they meet with failure. Pretending to be capable of great cunning or bravery, physical prowess, and even superhuman acts enables children to feel a sense of mastery and power over their surroundings. In the world of make-believe, at least, they are successful. A five-year-old may be land-bound, but Superman can fly!

Superhero play is useful as long as the children who are Superman, Batwoman, or Luke Skywalker do not become overexcited or hurt themselves or other children. When the teacher or parent becomes aware that a child is beginning to lose control, it is time to redirect the superhero into a quieter game. Building a Superman village, a space station, or a Batmobile out of blocks is one way of channeling the superhero energy into a constructive activity.

Submarine

YOU WILL NEED:

- map
- pretend submarine (e.g., large cardboard box)
- photographs of submarines and undersea divers
- pictures of sea creatures (e.g., dolphin, shark, whale, octopus)
- wooden or metal box
- treasure (e.g., costume jewelry, play money, foreign coins)

Talk to the children about submarines. Explain that submarines are ships that travel under the water instead of on its surface. Show photographs or models of submarines so the children have an idea of what a submarine looks like. Also, show pictures of the kinds of animals that live in the ocean, so the children can get a full sense of the fascinating environment of the deep.

Help the children create costumes for undersea diving. Then help them come up with a story line to get the action going. As everyone is piling into the submarine, which could be a large box or any enclosure, you might say something like this:

We have a map that shows where a ship sank to the bottom of the ocean a hundred years ago. Inside the ship is a treasure chest! With our submarine, we can go to the bottom of the ocean and find the treasure. Let's go!

Start engine number 1! Start engine number 2! Full speed ahead. Now, let's take the submarine below the surface, down, down, down, down. Feel the submarine roll back and forth as it travels down to the ocean floor.

The submarine is landing on the ocean floor. Let's climb out of the submarine in our diving suits, and swim to find the sunken ship. Swim like a fish, wiggle back and forth. Look at your map of the ocean floor. Where is the sunken ship? Look behind the rocks. (Demonstrate by *looking behind a piece of furniture.)* You find the ship! Fish are sleeping and swimming inside it. Count the fish: 1, 2, 3, 4, 5, 6, 7, 8, 9, 10. What colors are the fish? Blue, green, yellow, red, pink, purple.

Now we are searching for the treasure chest. Look! There it is! Open it! Look at all the beautiful jewels! Let's swim back to the submarine with the treasure. Everybody back into the submarine. It's time to go home.

After playing "submarine," you may want to build on the game with related activities. The children can draw fish, shells, and rocks seen in the ocean; make models of ocean creatures or a submarine with play dough; or go to the library and find books about the ocean or submarines.

Spaceship

YOU WILL NEED:

- **pretend spaceship (e.g., cushions or large cardboard box)**
- **photographs of astronauts in space suits, a space shuttle or rocket, the moon, and an outer-space view of the earth**

Explain that people can travel to the moon in spaceships. Show a model or picture of the space shuttle or a rocket. Show pictures of astronauts in space suits and introduce the term "astronaut." Tell the children that when they grow up they may be astronauts and actually go to the moon, and today they can prepare for the trip by pretending to go.

Help the children create astronaut costumes, which might involve bicycle helmets and paper towel rolls strapped to their backs. Everyone climbs into the spaceship (cushions arranged on the floor, or a long rectangular cardboard box) as you provide cues to get the game started:

Okay, astronauts, put on your seat belts. Now, turn on the engines. The engines are running. Begin the countdown. Everyone count with me: 10, 9, 8, 7, 6, 5, 4, 3, 2, 1, blast-off!!! *(Count slowly and encourage the children to call out the numbers with you or after you so that they can learn the concept of counting down.)* The spaceship is beginning to lift off the ground. Hear the engines roar! Feel the rocket shake as the spaceship goes up, up, up into the sky. Now we're out in space. Look down below. You see that beautiful blue and white ball? That's the earth! That's the way the earth looks from outer space. Now we're headed for the moon.

Now we are landing on the moon. Easy…easy… easy. Touchdown! Let's get out of the spaceship and explore the moon. It feels like we are walking in slow motion.

Let's get back into the spaceship to return home. Countdown to blast-off: 10, 9, 8, 7, 6, 5, 4, 3, 2, 1, blast-off!!! See how that blue and white ball is getting bigger as we get closer? We're almost there…touchdown! We're back on earth. Everyone is cheering because you were so brave. You were not afraid to go to the moon. One day you will go to the moon for real!

As always, get the game started and help out when the children need assistance, but otherwise let them run their show. It's possible that the story will go in directions that seem strange to you, but resist the temptation to steer the game back to the plot line you suggested. They will get more out of the game, in terms of both entertainment and education, if they pursue it in their own way.

After playing "spaceship," children usually enjoy related games, such as building a spaceship out of blocks or other materials; collecting "moon rocks"; drawing a picture of a spaceship, the moon, or the earth as seen from outer space; making medals for heroism out of construction paper. You can also visit the library and borrow many of the wonderful books for children about space travel.

Pirates

YOU WILL NEED:

- scarves or bandanas
- cardboard daggers
- eye pencil, face paint, or stage makeup
- pictures of pirates from children's books or magazines
- wooden or metal box
- treasure (e.g., costume jewelry, play money, foreign coins)
- toy shovels
- treasure map
- pretend ship (e.g., large cardboard box)

Before introducing the game, prepare a treasure of cheap costume jewelry, poker chips, play money, foreign coins from a trip abroad, and other items. Put the treasure in an old wooden or metal box (an old fruitcake tin works well), and bury it beneath soft dirt or leaves in the play area outdoors. Then draw a map that includes prominent features of the play area (a big tree, a boulder, a drain pipe) and shows the way to a buried treasure. You can increase the aged, authentic look of the map by wrinkling the paper and rubbing dirt on it.

Now introduce the game by explaining that pirates are tough sailors who navigate the seven seas looking for deserted islands where treasures have been buried. Show pictures of pirates from storybooks, and point out the clothes they wear. Then spend some time with the children making suitable costumes: scarves wrapped around the head, mustaches drawn on with eye pencil or stage makeup, daggers made of cardboard. Let the children get into their ship (a large cardboard box works well) and be on their way. As the game proceeds, let them discover the treasure map and suggest that they see if it really leads to buried treasure.

Pirates can also be played indoors on a rainy day, using toys and makeshift items to represent the sailors, ships, islands, sharks, and treasure in a sea of blue, which might be a blue bed sheet or rug. As the ships sail along, suggest adventures: a sailor falls overboard ("Look out for the shark! Throw him a line! Quick, pull him up!"); a terrible storm tosses the ship about and breaks the main mast; the ship takes on water ("Abandon ship! All hands to the life boat!"); the ship is drifting aimlessly on the ocean without food or water; and finally the ship washes up on an island, where the pirates find a treasure map and then the treasure (this time a box with snacks, hidden under a table or chair). Help them invent and sing a merry pirate song to celebrate their success.

CHAPTER EIGHT

Make–Believe Places: Environments for Pretend Play

artin and Lukas, ages two and three, sit on the floor of a small living room in a fourth-floor, inner-city walk-up. The children are supervised by their grandmother, who spends mornings with them while their mother, who waits tables at night, sleeps. Grandmother interacts with the children periodically, but mostly she is taking care of dishes and other chores, talking on the telephone, or watching television. There are few toys: an old soccer ball, some miniature toy soldiers and cars, a tin box full of broken crayons and chalk, and a large cardboard box that the TV came in.

These children are poor, and poverty is never welcome in any home. But the quality of their environment depends on many aspects that have not been described. Chief among these is the nature of the interactions between the boys and their grandmother. If she

encourages imaginative play, suggests story lines or characters, tells them stories, teaches them songs—then their environment may not be *intellectually* or *emotionally* impoverished. Indeed, insofar as the development of imagination is concerned, Martin and Lukas may be better off than some middle-class preschoolers who while away the same hours playing with expensive electronic toys.

Of course, we are not suggesting that poor children are better off than those who are more privileged. This scenario is meant to illustrate two points. First, the quality of a preschooler's environment has a profound effect on the child's cognitive development, especially where the development of imagination is concerned. Second, the developmental quality of a preschooler's environment cannot be assessed by adding up the dollar value of the items in it. In this chapter we discuss the physical environments in which preschoolers play, with an emphasis on encouraging pretend play and developing creativity. The good news is that it is possible for all teachers and parents, regardless of their resources, to put together a truly outstanding play area for their children.

THE INDOOR PLAY AREA

Create an area in your home or in the classroom that can become a special place for make-believe play. At home, this special place can be your child's bedroom, a corner of the living room or kitchen, part of your family room, or a specially designed children's playroom. If you are a preschool teacher, you may think of the entire classroom as a playroom.

The play area, wherever it is, should first of all be safe. "Safe" means no furniture that could tip over and injure a climbing child; no electric cords that are dangling or running across the floor or under a rug; no toxic substances; no unsupervised water sources such as toilets or sinks; no space heaters; nothing sharp or protruding to run into. Make sure the room is monitored by a working smoke detector.

The overall appearance of the room should be bright and cheerful, inviting play. It should be well-lit, preferably with windows and ceiling lights rather than table or pole lamps, which can tip over. A carpet or rug invites floor play more than hard surfaces. Ideally, the walls should be light in color to reflect light; pale hues of green, blue, yellow, peach, or pink are especially pleasing to the eye, and colorful prints and posters depicting scenes from nursery rhymes or adventure stories add even more vitality to the area. Once these fundamentals have been met, you have only to furnish the room.

Table and Chairs

A child-size table and chairs are basic equipment in a preschooler's play area. They are invaluable for tea parties, for playing "restaurant" or "school," for use as a receptionist's or nurse's desk, and for countless other functions. On its side, the table can become a horse stable, a mountain, or a puppet theater. With a sheet or blanket over it, it turns into an instant hideout. And, of course, it comes in handy for artwork, reading, and pretend play with miniature toys.

Children's table sets are available in a wide range of materials, from expensive solid wood to colorful and affordable molded plastic. You can also fashion a table and chairs from plastic or wooden crates and cartons, or build a table by securely attaching legs to an old solid-wood door. Even a cardboard carton, such as those that televisions and computers come in, makes a perfectly good table.

Storage

Adequate storage for toys is essential. If toy figures are scattered throughout the house and blocks are dumped into a toy chest full of dress-up clothes, dishes, animals, and trucks, children will resist digging out what they need and may abandon a game for lack of equipment. Similarly, if something can't be found because there is no regular place for it, a child can grow frustrated and lose interest in the game. Everything should have its place, and toys of a particular type should be stored together so they are accessible with minimal searching.

Elaborate storage equipment and containers in all shapes and sizes are sold everywhere, from specialty shops to discount stores to mail-order catalogs. Makeshift household items can serve the same function, though. Empty boxes and tins, for example, make good containers for miniature toys and art supplies. Larger cartons or sturdy shopping bags are ideal for such items as construction toys, blocks, and doll clothes.

Shelves are ideal homes for all of these containers, plus small trucks, books, stuffed animals and dolls, musical instruments, tape players and recordings, and other larger toys. Mark or partition the shelves so that there are separate units for each kind of item stored. This reduces clutter and makes it easier for the child to see exactly what is available.

Balls may be kept in an open crate or box in a corner. Dress-up clothes and costumes may be stored in another box or a hamper. A certain area of the room can be set aside as a parking lot for small vehicles, or they can be parked in a garage made of a cardboard box tipped on end.

When storage space is limited, one solution is to put some toys out of sight in an attic, basement, or closet for a time. Periodically, you can produce one or two of these items (often stirring great excitement) and store some other item that has lost its edge. By recycling toys in this way, there is less clutter in the playroom and more room to use the toys available.

Screens and Movable Walls

Another item that is often useful in a playroom is a three-panel screen. Used with simple props, it can be a puppet theater, a supermarket, a post office, a bank teller's window, a country cottage. An interesting feature of the screen is that it is rarely used by a single child; its very structure seems to demand at least two participants. Some models have extra features such as a window-type opening, chalkboard side panels, and a shelf. Those made of wood are sturdier, while cardboard versions are most affordable. If you're handy, you can easily make one using three interior plywood panels that are 3- or 4-foot square, fastened together with hinges, or just tape together three sheets of heavy cardboard. When you set up a screen, always be sure it is stable to prevent injuries.

Like screens, movable walls are also handy. Make one with a 4-foot-square piece of wallboard, framed by molding, and mounted on casters. The play area can be divided in any manner by these moving walls; a child can create a small room within a room. In a classroom, several of these dividers are ideal, but even a single one in a playroom gives a child privacy, as well as serving as a divider between a restaurant kitchen and dining room, a doctor's office and waiting room, or the king's chamber and the dragon's lair.

Optional Furnishings

Not much else in the way of furniture is needed. Space and budget permitting, a sofa and a large, upholstered chair provide comfortable resting spots for children listening to stories or taking naps. During pretend play, sofas and chairs become boats, mountains, boulders on a Martian landscape, a fort, or a place to hide when a dinosaur passes by. Comfortable, adult-size furniture also encourages the supervising adult to remain in the room, and gives adult visitors a place to sit. But if a sofa and chair are not practical, a bean bag or large cushions can serve nearly as well. Cushions can even be made out of old sheets, curtains, or fabric remnants stuffed with foam peanuts, rags, or other filler.

SPECIALTY AREAS

Consider setting aside areas of the playroom for particular materials and activities. Any part of the room can be designated for a special function, as long as it is identified in some way (for example, by putting a colored-tape line on the floor). Because corners are especially handy for this, such areas are often called specialty corners. The specialty corners you create should reflect the interests of your children. In deciding what specialty areas to establish, let your children guide you. If an art corner doesn't get used much, convert it into something more productive. If the child shows a strong interest in flying machines, set up an airport and suspend model planes, gliders, and spaceships from the ceiling, keeping them high enough so that they don't pose a hazard to young pilots walking by. Here are a few ideas:

HOUSE CORNER

Most children enjoy playing "house," and most of the materials required are ordinary and inexpensive household items. Cardboard boxes can be fashioned into stoves, refrigerators, and other appliances, as well as tables and chairs; a quilt on the floor with pillows and blankets makes a fine bed; cushions can be a sofa or living room chairs. A small broom or large whisk broom, dustpan, and rags should be available to play "clean-up" with. A few purchases that get long mileage in pleasure include tea sets, miniature pots and pans, a toy telephone, and a toy vacuum cleaner. Additional equipment for playing house can be scavenged from household drawers, kitchen cabinets, and closets.

Dollhouses lend themselves to make-believe house play. If they have open sides or an open top, the small child can easily manipulate the play people and possessions he or she chooses to use. If the walls are unadorned, the child can become an instant decorator by making paintings on index cards or adhesive notes, and rugs cut from fabric pieces.

DRESS-UP CORNER

Children love to dress up in strange clothes. They especially like to don daddy and mommy clothes, but they also enjoy wearing the garb of other adults, people who are more glamorous and exotic, workers in uniform, and superheroes.

Keep a box with scarves, shoes, jackets, dresses, shirts, vests, and accessories, including hats—lots of hats. A hat is a wondrous item of apparel. An old bonnet, hood, beret, or fedora can lead a child to assume roles of babies, artists, detectives, nursery rhyme and fairy tale characters, and moms and dads. You can purchase ready-made costumes for children, but they are not necessary—or even desirable, since they take away the child's opportunity to imagine and create an original design.

Many items can be borrowed from the hand-me-downs of older children and adults; others can be constructed from simple household materials. A sheriff's badge, for instance, can be made with a pair of scissors, some cardboard, and aluminum foil; a dish towel becomes a Batman cape. An old negligee becomes a beautiful ball gown, and a discarded white shirt makes a fine uniform for a doctor, dentist, nurse, or waitress, as well as an artist's smock. Scarves suggest multiple uses. In general, old clothes lend themselves to improvisation, and many of these dress-up articles endure for years.

Makeup can offer a young child endless delight. Whether it is a mustache or scar drawn with a bit of charcoal, or the comic look of a clown, children find the conversion of their faces into those of pirates, cowhands, gypsies, and royalty great fun. A mirror in which to view the metamorphosis is essential. A thin layer of cold cream under the artwork helps ease cleansing later on.

SCIENCE CORNER

Most children are curious about the natural environment. Set aside an area where they can collect and explore plants, rocks, bird nests, dried leaves, berries, snake skins, seeds, potting soil, and the like. Such items are useful when you help the children learn about the different senses—sight, touch, smell, hearing. Keep a magnifying glass in the area for inspecting the items, and show the children how wetting an object can change its odor and feel. Keep seashells on hand for "listening to the ocean." You might also have maps posted on the wall. Maps of the playroom, the playground if there is one, and the immediate neighborhood are probably more valuable than maps of the state, country, or world.

Small animals such as gerbils, hamsters, white mice, and goldfish can have their place in the science corner, especially in a classroom. If you're willing to accept the odor and mess, let the children learn to feed the animals and help clean the cages. Animals provide an opportunity to love and care for another being. Children love their stuffed animals, so this is a good place to make the transition from pretend to reality. Children are also less likely to develop animal phobias if they have had positive experiences with animals. And the animals can be incorporated into make-believe play: A caged gerbil can be used in puppet shows as the enchanted creature who changes into the hand puppet prince or princess, and a goldfish in a small bowl is a wonderful prop for a pirate game.

Constructing a science corner can be as easy as putting up a display shelf, with small items such as seashells and stones stored in shoe boxes or tins. An old chest of drawers, preferably one that is child-size, provides storage for a more extensive collection. Identify each drawer's contents with a word and appropriate picture on the outside. One drawer might be devoted to bird eggs and nests, another to sea shells, another to flowers. The drawers can be partitioned (eggs in one section, nests in another) with pieces of stiff cardboard. Try not to let the collection become stale. Encourage the children to find new rocks, new shells, new objects of every kind: a feather, a piece of bark, a pine cone.

ANIMAL ALERT

Having animals in the playroom means there is the potential for animal abuse. Because of this, you may choose not to have them. If you do have small animals for your children, keep in mind that children who systematically abuse animals are often troubled, according to research. Some of these children are themselves victims of physical or psychological abuse. Moreover, children who deliberately hurt animals are later likely to abuse other children.

If you see a pattern of mistreatment of animals in a child, be alert to the possibility that the child is mistreated in some way, and spend extra time with him as he interacts with animals. This will allow you to observe him more closely and, importantly, allow you to demonstrate the proper treatment and provide praise when he handles animals correctly. In this way, you may do both the animal and the abusive child a great service.

Of course, if you do suspect mistreatment or abuse, confer with your director, school counselor, pediatrician, or other appropriate professional, and follow up as deemed neccessary through proper channels.

ART CORNER

Children can work on art projects at the main table in the play area, or you may want to have an art corner. Here you might set up a small table and chair, an easel, a drop cloth (an old shower curtain or plastic tarp) to protect the floor, smocks (old adult shirts), play dough, pencils, charcoal, crayons, drawing or scrap paper, paints, brushes, rags for cleaning spills, and a plastic basin for water for cleaning brushes, hands, and smudged faces. You might also have a blackboard, chalk, and erasers. Supplies should be kept on shelves, with smaller items (such as crayons) stored separately in small tins or boxes.

HIDEOUT CORNER

Children enjoy enclosed hideaways. Large kitchen appliance boxes are ideal for this purpose. Fold the flaps of one end inside and position the box on its side in a corner, with the end open to the room. Alternatively, drape an old sheet or curtain from a card table or other frame. Place a rug inside, or a couple of cushions, and supply a flashlight. These spaces conjure make-believe play involving caves, igloos, forts, tents, and such, in addition to providing a relaxing retreat for book browsing (with good lighting) or simple privacy.

OTHER SPECIALTY AREAS

There are, of course, other kinds of special corners you may want to create, depending on your own interests and those of the children. Adults with a high tolerance for noise may, for example, set up a music corner, with toy drums and other instruments, pots and pans, penny whistles, an ocarina, a toy horn, a kazoo. Paper towel rolls become brass trumpets once their use is demonstrated by an adult. A tape player enables a crooner to sing along with professionals. See "Do-It-Yourself Band" on page 71 for more ideas.

Another specialty area might be a library, with appropriate volumes arranged on shelves. The library might be combined with the hideaway, with book shelves or a book case under the hideaway's roof or outside its door. A cushion on the floor provides a comfortable place to sit while looking at the books.

TOYS FOR THE PLAYROOM

Certain toys are especially likely to excite the preschooler's imagination. Indeed, one of the joys of being a parent or teacher is watching the delight of a child who has been transported into some wondrous imaginary time and place by a doll, a tin soldier, or a model plane. What makes for a good toy? The best satisfy three S's: They are safe, sturdy, and stimulating.

Safety is the first consideration in evaluating any toy. Examine toys for sharp edges or points, slippery surfaces, flaking paint, splinters, small parts that can be swallowed, and toxic substances. Toys that children are likely to climb on (even if such treatment is not intended) should be strong enough to bear much more than the weight of the heaviest child. Despite our best efforts, there is probably no such thing as a completely child-proof toy, though. A child can slip on a small block left on the floor, or get poked in the eye with a paintbrush. Our responsibility as adults is to monitor children as they play and intervene when the risks become unacceptable.

After safety, consider sturdiness. Children's toys are their possessions. A birthday present that fails to perform or breaks while a child is still discovering what it's all about is a crushing disappointment—and may even cause injury. Elaborate (and often expensive) battery-operated toys that quickly break down are particularly disappointing. Sometimes sturdier toys can be more costly, but their durability can make them a better value over less expensive counterparts, which may have to be repaired or replaced.

Finally, be aware that toys vary in how much they stimulate pretend play. Jigsaw puzzles, board games, and number and word games are all invaluable tools for developing academic and cognitive skills, but they don't stir a child's imagination. Good pretend toys tend to be simple. Generally speaking, the more a toy does, the less it requires from the child's imagination and the less it stimulates pretend play. The best toys for pretend play can be used by the child for many purposes. A jigsaw puzzle, for example, is *nothing but* a jigsaw puzzle. A scrap of fabric, on the other hand, can be a magician's cape, a pirate's hat, a cowpoke's scarf, a waiter's towel, a bandit's mask, a cook's apron, a bride's veil, a lady's purse, a gentleman's handkerchief, a surgeon's bandage—the list is infinite. The more ways a child can use an item, the more ways she will.

Of course, the toy that stimulates pretend play in a two-year-old may not work with a four-year-old, and vice versa. A Barbie doll in a wedding gown suggests a narrow range of play, but this suggestion may be just what the three-year-old needs to enter the world of make-believe. The five-year-old, on the other hand, may find such specific toys constricting, and may prefer a more generic doll dressed in street clothes who can take on a number of roles. Nevertheless, in general, toys that are simple and ambiguous are preferable to those that are complex and specific. Here are several items that make effective pretend toys.

Household Items

Children love to play with grown-up things. A hand-operated egg-beater, plastic containers, pots, aprons, a small broom, and such make useful props in playing "house." Tools that are safe for children such as a tape measure and small wrenches are fun for playing "carpenter." Macaroni and cut-up drinking straws can be strung together into bracelets and necklaces, and pipe cleaners can be made into dolls, animals, and geometric forms. Everything from buttons to popcorn to magazine covers is material for art projects. Cardboard tubes from toilet paper and paper towels make good horns and telescopes, telephones and pirate spyglasses.

Blocks

Building blocks are basic. They can be used to construct a farm, a dollhouse, a skyscraper, a zoo, a network of roads, a fire station, an entire village. Their possibilities are limited only by the number available and the imagination and manipulative skills of the children. Be sure to include some large blocks in your set, and those shaped like wedges, arches, tunnels, and cylinders. Wood blocks are marketed in a wide range of prices, depending on the hardness of the wood, the size and number of blocks, and the variety of shapes in the set. A set of top-quality blocks will last indefinitely and remain in continuous use in a family or a nursery school, so investing in such a set is usually worthwhile.

Several companies now manufacture large rectangular blocks made of sturdy cardboard. Purchased as flat sheets with detailed folding instructions, they rely on the egg-carton principle for their

strength: a single block can hold up to 200 pounds. Because of their light weight and large size, they frequently become cars and trains for children to ride on, sofas and beds for them to lounge on, garages and farms for parking and corralling animals, or small houses in which to hide.

Colorful plastic bricks or logs that interlock have the advantage of rigidity. That is, the maze of animal cages or the fleet of ambulances that a child constructs with them cannot easily be destroyed by a baby sister who is learning to crawl or a Batman who sweeps through the room. Also, these blocks are highly portable. Since they are small, hundreds can be slipped into a small cardboard box when the family goes on vacation or the child faces a long wait somewhere. The addition of a few miniature people or vehicles can extend their play value greatly.

Boxes

The versatile box is a simple but mighty addition to the playroom. Small boxes can become cars and trucks. A set of them positioned end to end becomes a train. Attach a toilet paper tube to one box, and you have an engine with a smoke stack. Remove the lids of the other boxes and put crayons, cotton balls, and any other small items in them, and you have a freight train; restore the lids and draw windows on the sides and you have a passenger train.

Shoe boxes make good medical kits, miniature lions' cages, and vehicles. Topless shoe boxes form the rooms of a hotel, beds for plush animals and dolls, or the play toasters in a restaurant game. A round oatmeal box is a castle tower, a cannon, a lighthouse; cut it in half lengthwise and you have two boats or a pair of watering troughs for cattle on the farm.

Larger boxes make a fine desk, or a play stove, sink, or refrigerator. Appropriate knobs or dials can be drawn on the box.

The largest boxes, from major kitchen appliances, can serve as a house, post office, store, or puppet stage. Adults can cut out doors and windows. (If you make the windows round and outline squares around them with marking pens, you will retain the strength of the structure.) Positioned on its side, it makes a fine hideaway (see "Specialty Areas," above).

Toy Vehicles

Cars, buses, trucks, road graders, dump trucks, steam shovels, trains, motorcycles, airplanes, and boats intrigue young children, who often find magic in movement. Miniature vehicles are useful with blocks and other structures; medium-sized vehicles can carry dolls, animals, and cargo, and are particularly easy for the small child to manipulate.

Large vehicles in which children can ride themselves give a sense of power to rule the world. A riding truck, suitable for zooming around indoors or out, can enliven countless situations. It is alternately a car driving to the library, a rocket going to the moon, or a motorcycle heading for California.

Stationary vehicles, boxlike in structure but with room for two to five children, come equipped with one or more steering wheels and their own possibilities. They are expensive and space-consuming for home use, but their equivalent can be constructed easily from cardboard or improvised by lining up a few chairs or laying large blocks or cushions end to end.

Dolls and Stuffed Animals

The tremendous variety of dolls and stuffed animals on the market attests to their popularity among children. When no one is around to play the role of baby, sick patient, villain, or admiring audience, a doll or stuffed animal can fill the bill. It can become a companion or an adversary, be tended to or attacked, and take on all manner of personalities, depending on what the child requires at the moment.

In selecting dolls and stuffed animals, remember that the less the toy does, the more conducive it will be to make-believe play. The child who decides what words a doll will utter and in which voice, or where and how the doll will move, is in true control of the script. Movable limbs are useful; battery-powered vocabularies are not. The centuries-old rag doll and modern factory or homemade variations continue to charm their way into the play lives of young children.

Puppets

Puppets give the child another voice. Many children are willing to let a puppet experiment with new words and ideas, express concerns, and take other risks that they themselves would not be willing to take. It is the puppet who expresses anger or fear or jealousy, for example, not the puppeteer, or so the child seems to think. Perhaps because of this, the child's willingness to use them often depends on the willingness of adults to participate.

Puppets may resemble familiar cartoon or television figures, fairy tale characters, soldiers and sailors, fierce or cuddly animals, ordinary people and superheroes, angels and monsters. Some are small enough for one finger, others large enough for the entire hand. Each type has its own advantages and disadvantages, but those that require moving the puppet's head with one or two fingers are too difficult for the young child to handle and should be avoided. Puppets of every type can be purchased in toy stores or special puppet shops; however, very functional puppets can be made at home from discarded socks or mittens, sticks, paper bags, cardboard tubes, or sponges.

Miniature Toys and Play Environments

Miniature human figures, including family members and people in uniforms such as soldiers and astronauts, are vital to any make-believe toy collection. Miniature people can be store-bought or home-made, by painting faces and clothing on plastic or wooden spools, wooden ice cream spoons, and even small blocks and popsicle sticks. Also include animals, furniture, and other miniature accessories in the collection.

There are many miniature play environments on the market, including plastic and cardboard airports, farms, zoos, arks, ranches, restaurants, gas stations, and garages, which usually come complete with their own suitably uniformed miniature people, such as gas station attendants, pilots, flight attendants, and cooks. Much more structured than child-designed or improvised environments using blocks and boxes, these environments can be a stimulant to children just beginning to build their make-believe skills. Care should be taken, however, to select toys that are very sturdy, and give preference to those with a handy place for storing the accessories.

While miniature environments can be purchased, you can also build simple yet appealing versions out of scrap lumber. And a variation on the instant-environment theme is the ever-useful length of sturdy fabric, such as an oilcloth. Available in a wide range of colors at low cost, an oilcloth can be spread out on the floor as a sea for pirates and their ships, a desert for Indians to traverse, or a terrain for a maze of roads or apartment buildings. Roads, buildings, lakes, and other features can be drawn or sewn on.

Make Your Own Play Dough

YOU WILL NEED:

- 2 cups flour
- 1 cup salt
- Water
- Cooking oil
- 1 tablespoon distilled white vinegar
- Baby powder
- Food coloring

It's easy to make your own play dough. Measure two cups of flour into a mixing bowl and add one cup of salt. Little by little, add water until the mixture is just moist but not wet. Add a drop of cooking oil to make the dough smooth, and a tablespoon of vinegar to retard spoilage. Sprinkle in some fine baby powder to improve the dough's odor, and several drops of food coloring.

Knead the dough until it is uniform in consistency and appearance, then wrap it in plastic and store it in a refrigerator until a few hours before it will be used. Making play dough is an excellent rainy day activity for children. The kneading of the dough is fine exercise for their finger muscles, and making something they will later use is good for their sense of pride.

Art Supplies

Two items are a must for all preschoolers: crayons and play dough. Crayons are an economical and unmessy medium for creating colorful pictures, and they come in more colors than a child can sometimes count! A new box of 8 or 16 or 64 is always exciting. The crayons that have one flat side to prevent them from rolling off the table are ideal for this age. Play dough is for three-dimensional creations. It is non-toxic, colorful, and easy to use for little hands and fingers as they pound, roll, and squeeze it into balls, coils, and more complex forms, including baskets, animals, dolls, cars, and people.

Finger paints provide tactile and creative pleasure even for the youngest child, and the paint can be removed from floor, face, and clothing easily. Paper for coloring and painting may be large sheets and tablets of inexpensive newsprint, shelving paper, or special finger paint paper. Tempera paints, felt-tip markers, watercolors, and squeeze paints that come in small tubes with felt stoppers are suitable for slightly

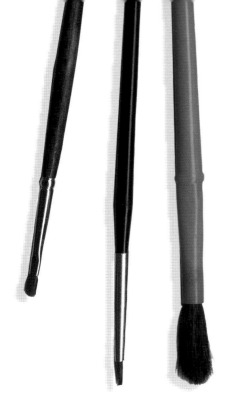

older preschoolers. Clean-up is more difficult than with crayons and finger paint, so these items are best reserved for children ages three and above. Paintbrushes in a range of thicknesses are fun to experiment with. In addition to paintbrushes, consider using feathers, a lambswool roller, or a brayer (a special roller for spreading ink).

A collection of colored chalk sticks is great fun for all ages on a chalkboard, or outdoors on a sidewalk or exterior wall. Stamps and stamp pads are also a treat, especially if the stamps come in the shapes of animals, humans, and cartoon figures, letters, or numbers. An art supplies collection should also include glitter, glue and glue sticks, pipe cleaners, and a wide variety of scrap materials such as popsicle sticks, feathers, crepe paper, and ribbon.

THE OUTDOOR PLAY AREA

Fresh air, sunshine, trees, clouds, the sights and sounds of birds and animals, and the room to run free—these are the things that a child can revel in outdoors. An outdoor play area, such as a backyard, park, or playground, can be thought of as a playroom without a roof.

The perfect outdoor area is fenced or has a natural enclosure of bushes or hedges at the perimeter to keep children from wandering away, discourage trespassers, and give the children (and their parents and teachers) the feeling of a safe, cozy place in which to play. A small hill and one or more large trees for shade and for a swing are bonus features that add to the enjoyment, and a sunny area is useful if you would like to grow a small flower or vegetable garden with your children. Add a bench and table in the play area for any visiting or supervising adults.

As always, safety is the first priority. Walk the play area from time to time to make sure that no dangers have crept in, such as broken glass, trash, fallen tree branches, exposed wires or cables, animal waste, standing water, or holes in the ground that a child could lose his footing in.

A blessing in itself, an outdoor play area can be enhanced by toys that encourage pretend play. Many commonplace toys and other items make good outdoor playthings, including smooth planks of wood, old tires, pots and pans, child-sized rakes and shovels, and jump ropes. Here are more suggestions that will transform your play area into a zone rich with make-believe possibilities.

Sandbox

Sand offers myriad opportunities for imaginative play. The footprints children make in sand can become the marks of a dinosaur. Feet and legs can be buried until they disappear, and then emerge as if by magic. Cakes and pies and cookies can be "baked" in plastic and metal containers of all shapes and decorated with sticks, stones, and shells. Old spoons and forks can help create intricate roadways; buckets or margarine containers become elaborate buildings. A two-foot shovel may be useful for excavation at the beach; a few construction trucks help in engineering projects.

Sand needs to be contained in some way, and there are many options. The traditional sandbox can be built from four pressure-treated 2-by-12-inch planks, arranged in a square or rectangle and embedded 4 to 6 inches in the ground. Consider the number of children who may use the box at any one time before deciding on the size of the box.

The basic sandbox can be improved at little extra cost. A cement floor will keep young excavators from mixing topsoil with the sand. A hinged cover over the box keeps the sand dry and free of twigs and leaves, and deters neighborhood pets from soiling the sand.

Traditional sandboxes serve children very well, but with a little imagination you may find a more stimulating container. One of the most delightful is a derelict rowboat. The seats not only provide a place for the sailors, but serve to keep children's sand constructions separate if they so desire. The boat itself has obvious play possibilities.

Dirt Pile

Outdoor play must include mention of good old-fashioned dirt. A dirt pile may seem a strange or unattractive addition to the play area, but grown-ups will find that with child-size shovels on hand, youngsters turn themselves into construction crews, campers, buried-treasure hunters, and farmers. Digging dirt is also demanding work, and the child permitted to master its challenge is likely to feel strong and proud. If the child is helped to develop interesting plot lines and make-believe games, there is less likelihood that the dirt will merely get thrown at the house or at other children.

Water World

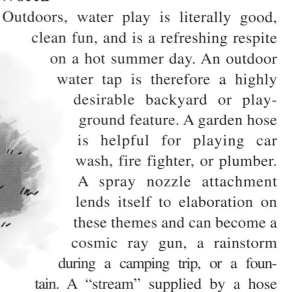

Outdoors, water play is literally good, clean fun, and is a refreshing respite on a hot summer day. An outdoor water tap is therefore a highly desirable backyard or playground feature. A garden hose is helpful for playing car wash, fire fighter, or plumber. A spray nozzle attachment lends itself to elaboration on these themes and can become a cosmic ray gun, a rainstorm during a camping trip, or a fountain. A "stream" supplied by a hose provides the opportunity to pan for gold, irrigate a miniature farm, or build a bridge or dam.

A wading pool is a place for sea divers, for sailing to China, or a space shuttle splashdown. Similarly, a galvanized wash tub provides an ocean for toy ships and rafts or a place to wash doll clothes or small cars and trucks on very hot days. A tub of water can also be set inside an old tire to make an interesting marina or moat. A bucket of water with a wide paintbrush enables a child to paint fences, houses, cars. A few drops of dishwashing detergent in the bucket changes the water to a witches brew.

Be sure to empty any water containers each evening for safety and to avoid creating breeding places for mosquitoes.

CAUTION!

Any water play, especially involving wading pools and other containers, requires continuous adult supervision.

Pet Corner

A pet rabbit in a cage might make a nice addition to the play area. As noted earlier, children like to pet and feed animals, and the care and nurturing of a small creature helps a child understand nature and develop some sense of responsibility. With adult modeling, instruction, and supervision, animals also help teach children kindness. If you do have a rabbit, you'll need to provide an indoor home for it when the weather gets colder. To keep the animal from being injured or lost, be sure that the children cannot remove it from the cage without adult help.

Boxes and Barrels

The box, which serves children so well indoors, is perhaps the most versatile of all outdoor playthings. A box that is open at one end and large enough for a child to crawl into can be all the things it is when used indoors, including houses, tents, mountains, and stages. On snowy days, a box can become an igloo or a snow fort. Smaller boxes serve as stools, work tables, dining tables, desks, and more specific items such as a judge's bench. Plastic and wooden boxes are, of course, far more durable than cardboard and can be left outdoors. Wood boxes will last longer in the elements if they are painted or constructed of pressure-treated lumber.

Barrels are also a barrel of fun. An empty oak whiskey barrel tipped on its side and rocking can be a galloping horse to ride across the plains. If the lid is removed, it becomes a moving cave or a hide-out. Standing on the barrel's curved side helps to develop leg muscles and transports the child to the circus, where he performs a miraculous balancing act. Plastic barrels such as those that store farm products are lighter in weight than oak barrels and brightly colored, but never use those that contained toxic chemicals, and always wash them out thoroughly before turning them over to children.

An alternative to the barrel is a length of large drainage piping, at least 36 inches in diameter, which suggests countless uses in pretend play. Children enjoy crawling through an enclosed and mildly scary place. Purchase plastic piping, rather than galvanized metal, because it is safer to play in and lighter—and hence easier to move. It is available at building supply stores.

Riding Vehicles

Wagons, platform trucks, scooters, child-size wheelbarrows, and especially tricycles are even more fun outside than indoors. Provide as many different vehicles as space and budget considerations will permit. A tricycle can take a doctor on her rounds, a grown-up to work, or a police officer to the scene of a robbery. A wagon can be an ambulance transporting an injured person to the hospital, a truck carrying troops or supplies to the front lines, or a circus wagon carrying lions and tigers. It can help the newspaper boy or girl make deliveries, the lumberjack carry logs, mom or dad do the grocery shopping, and the hunter carry the prey back to camp. A group of children with vehicles can form a wagon train headed west to settle a new land, or a convoy heading for Alaska, or a scientific expedition exploring the barren surface of the moon.

Swings

A swing is a basic feature of most playgrounds, and a nice option in your own play area. Children can mount them and go to Mars, pretend they are on a ride at an amusement park, make believe they are flying, or be circus acrobats on a trapeze.

Make sure the swing is off to the side of the play area, where other children are not passing by, and that there is adult supervision. The seat of a preschooler's swing should be a foot above the ground and hung on about five feet of rope. (The length of the rope determines the height the seat can reach while swinging, and hence the distance the child can fall.) Be sure that the rope is attached to a large, healthy tree branch or to a sturdy metal swing frame. The swing rope should be of a material that can stand up to moisture and sunlight. Check it regularly for signs of wear, and test the strength of a swing by sitting on it yourself. The swing seat can be made of

canvas, plastic, or light wood. An old small tire (not a large truck tire, which is heavy) also serves well. Metal and hardwoods are not good choices, because the risk of injury is greater should a child be hit.

Slide

A slide is another traditional playground item that becomes a good source of pretend play. You can find a wide variety of plastic slides on the market, suitable for both indoor and outdoor use and small enough to be safe for preschoolers. Many slides are part of more elaborate play structures. In make-believe play, a slide quickly becomes an escape hatch, a fire fighter's pole, or a mountain; even the space beneath is rich with pretend possibilities.

Seesaw

Several current versions of the seesaw are made of molded plastic, and can be used both indoors and out. Made in widths designed to hold one or two children on either end, seesaws suggest boats, buses, and stagecoaches.

Climbing Equipment

Climbing and shimmying up and down quickly become the impetus for a make-believe game. Poles and ropes for climbing are also a good source of physical exercise. At least 18 inches of a 4- or 5-foot pole embedded in cement should be underground. A step stool near the pole helps the child get up to the top for the slide down. A knotted rope or rope ladder suspended from a sturdy tree branch provides an alternative to the climbing pole. More elaborate and expensive climbing structures or jungle gyms can be considered if the playground budget permits. The space under even the simplest of these structures can be a makeshift clubhouse, prison, or fort.

Playhouse

Young children who are fortunate enough to have a playhouse often consider it the ultimate of outdoor playthings. There is a special excitement for a child who can crawl or climb into a small enclosed space and be in a world of his own. Whether it is a simple shell structure or an elaborate log cabin, the playhouse provides a perfect setting for all sorts of dramatic play. Within the freedom of their private preserve, children let their imaginations go. The playhouse becomes the fort, clubhouse, store, cave, island hut, pirate's den, castle, teepee, frontier cabin, and witch's home. It also offers the child a special place to be alone for a moment, an opportunity that is essential to the child's growth and well-being.

SAFETY FIRST—AGAIN

As with indoor toys, safety, sturdiness, and the ability to stimulate pretend play are the key assets of a good outdoor toy. Outdoor playthings tend to move in unpredictable ways, and the heavier a moving object is, the more dangerous it is. A seesaw made of thick hardwood is very sturdy, but if it comes down on a child's head it can cause serious injury. A swing with a seat made of durable oak or metal may last for decades, but its weight makes it a potentially dangerous missile. Toys made of molded plastic are light, free of sharp corners and splinters, and resistant to the elements. A good rule of thumb in selecting an outdoor plaything that moves is to get the one made of the lightest material. Durability is nice; safety is essential.

Also remember, however, that an absolutely safe environment is not achievable and, if achieved, would probably be very boring! If children are to get the most out of outdoor play, they must have a measure of freedom, which entails risk. The role of the parent and the teacher is to watch, weigh the risks of an activity against the benefits, and intervene when necessary. §

CHAPTER NINE

Special Games for Special Times

Three-year-old Tim is with his dad on a trip to the zoo that has been unaccountably interrupted by a stop at the bank. They have been standing in line for what seems like forever, and all he can think about are the lions, monkeys, and ice cream cones that he is missing. "Can we go now?" he asks for the tenth time. "In a minute," his father says once again. With nothing to take his mind off the frustration of waiting, Tim is growing cranky and difficult.

Meanwhile, Tim's four-year-old sister Katie is in bed with a sore throat. She has been there all morning, and has read almost every book in her own library—twice. Now she wants something different to do. She wants to be with her brother at the zoo, or go to her neighbor Marcus's birthday party, but her mother says she has to stay put and get well. She is bored and starting to whine.

And next door, Marcus is excited about being five years old and having a birthday party, but he is also uneasy. Sometimes parties aren't very much fun, he is remembering, especially when you lose all the games, or when someone else gets great presents that you are not allowed to play with.

Like all preschoolers, Tim, Katie, and Marcus have little experience with settings and situations outside of the ordinary and familiar. Both inside and outside the home, there is much that can seem strange, confusing, worrisome, or boring. In these troublesome circumstances, make-believe games are the ideal solution, in no small part because the play situation is almost completely under the child's control—when everything else around him is not.

The games described in this chapter are designed to help children develop a repertoire of diversions or techniques that can be drawn upon in those periods of restlessness or stress that all youngsters inevitably confront. Waiting in itself is difficult for many children; the confusion of sights and sounds in a supermarket or other bustling public place can be stressful for others; in a doctor's office, fear added to restlessness can make for an especially difficult time. Parties, especially when one child is the focus of attention, can strain children's patience. Even bath time can be scary for some children, or simply going off to sleep at night in a darkened room. Then, of course, there are those sick-in-bed days when the hours drag on in the isolation of the bedroom. Here, then, are some ways that imagination can shine some light in the darker corners of a child's day. §

GAMES WORTH WAITING FOR

All of us, children and adults alike, often find ourselves in situations that require waiting. Waiting rooms, check-out lines, lengthy car rides—all of these are particularly trying for children. A preschooler likes to be physically active, to move around, to explore the environment. These youngsters lack the adult's capacity for reading alone or losing themselves in thought, so they often start to squirm or fuss or get into mischief. But the child who has skill with make-believe play and a few simple toys—small blocks, little people, miniature cars—can quickly create an elaborate game that keeps him entertained and out of trouble.

Waiting Bag

YOU WILL NEED:

- **fabric sack with closure**
- **assortment of small, simple toys**
- **assortment of craft materials**

Keep a small bag of playthings to take along when you are going to have to wait with a child in tow. Tell your child that this is a special "waiting bag" to be used only when he is on an outing and needs something special to amuse himself. Long automobile trips and airplane flights, as well as time spent in waiting rooms, will be much more pleasant.

The toys and games should be relatively simple, small, and adaptable. A variety of small plastic figures of animals, people, and props are good to have. Include small cars, small blocks, and some simple craft materials that will not require clean-up, such as pipe cleaners, crayons, play dough, and pads of paper.

Suggest themes to your child, and include the toys needed to support those ideas in the waiting bag. Help your child with simple plots and dialogue for each situation, as needed. Once the game is under way, children are usually able to continue by themselves, but if the game begins to falter you might comment on some feature of the game ("My, what a fancy hotel this is. How does this elevator work?") or suggest a challenging event ("What's happening? The space ship is going through a meteor shower! Meteors are hitting the ship! Captain, what should we do?"). Here are some themes and a list of the toys needed to support them:

FERRY BOAT
The child is the ferry boat master and must see that passengers are boarded and conveyed across a river or bay. The toy bag should include some small boats or blocks, blue fabric or paper for water, and miniature plastic people (or pipe cleaners, wooden clothespins, etc.) for passengers.

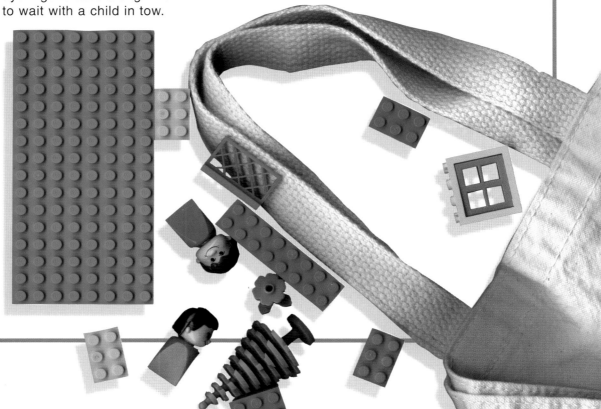

KING AND QUEEN

The child can pretend to be the king or queen of an imaginary country. If the situation permits, someone else—a parent, a sibling, a friend—can be the princess, dragon, court jester, or other role that the child suggests or the children agree on. The toy bag should include small blocks (for construction of a castle), miniature people, horses, and perhaps a magician or dragons, which your child might make out of play dough.

SPACE TRIP

Suggest that you and your child are waiting to board a space ship for a trip to a mysterious planet. The bag should include a small rocket ship, blocks to build structures on the planet, miniature people to be astronauts or inhabitants of the planet, and materials to make alien creatures and scenery.

HOTEL

The child may pretend to have his very own hotel. He will need small blocks for the front desk and furniture, a small box for an elevator, miniature figures to represent bellhops, a desk clerk, guests, and waiters. Provide colored paper to be used for plants, signs, and other details.

FARM

Your child can set up her own farm with stables, pastures, a barn, farm house, horses, sheep, and other animals. Include animal figures, building blocks, small vehicles, and pieces of fabric to serve as fields, plus people figures to be farmers, stable hands, and riders.

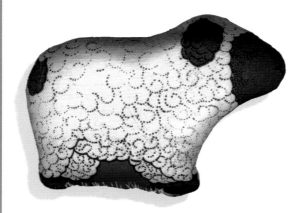

Explorer

All children like to explore. If you're stuck waiting in a lobby, terminal, or line—virtually anywhere—ask your child to be an explorer and find things in the immediate surroundings. If your child knows the various colors, ask her to find something in the room that is blue, red, green, black, and so on. If she knows the basic shapes, ask her to find something that is round, or square, or triangular. You can make the game more complex by combining two concepts, such as color and shape or color and size; for example, find something small and red, or round and blue. This may be a bit of a challenge for four- and five-year-olds; move on to another game if the child cannot be successful most of the time. If it isn't practical to have the child moving around the room, ask her to call out or point to the item.

Word Games

Simple word games can be played with five-year-olds and some four-year-olds.

- Ask the child to name a word that rhymes with a word you provide. Begin with one-syllable nouns, such as "bed," "shoe," "house," and "toy." Start by offering some examples.

- Ask the child to provide a word that begins with a certain letter or sound. "Give me a word that starts with *D* as in door," or "What's a word that starts with *M* as in monkey?"

- Some preschoolers, when given a word, can provide its opposite. Say, "If I'm not small, I'm____" or "If I'm not cold, I'm ____" and let the child complete the sentence.

- An easy word game involves asking the child to name short words, such as "can," "do," or "bug." If that proves too easy, ask the child to think of a long word, such as "kangaroo," "umbrella," or "dinosaur." Give your child examples to get her started.

Keeping score with any of these games may help keep the game going and be a source of pride for the child. However, if more than one child is playing, it may spur rivalry and be counterproductive.

Car Games

Children can play these games on their own or with the participation of an adult to help pass the time during a long car ride.

LICENSE PLATES

Explain to your child that cars coming from different places have license plates that are different colors. If your child is old enough to understand the concept "states," so much the better. Have him look for license plates that are different colors or come from different states, and call them out as he sees them. You can carry this a step further by suggesting that the child make up a story about the people in some of the cars, where they have come from, where they are going, and what they will do there.

CARS IN COMMON

Have your child point out cars of a particular color, such as red. Each time he sees a red car, he wins a point. Variations include cars with animal passengers (especially good in summer, when the roads are full of vacationers traveling with pets) or cars with a trailer or boat in tow.

SIGNS

Play the classic alphabet game by having the child search for signs containing the letters of the alphabet, in order from A to Z. On a long trip this is a satisfying game and a fun way to introduce preschoolers to reading. If your child is beginning to read, suggest that he look for signs that say "stop," "food," "exit," "detour," "gas," "toll," and so on. You can also have your child pick a number such as 7 and count how many signs he sees with that number in five or ten minutes; on longer trips do this with all numbers 1 through 9 and keep a list to compare the frequency.

Guessing Games

Children enjoy games in which they guess the solution to a kind of riddle. One of you makes the sound of a train, horn, telephone, church bell, or some animal, and the other has to guess what is being imitated. Start the game with the adult making the first sound, then take turns.

Songs

Songs are a great source of entertainment. Children generally love to sing, especially when others are singing with them. Here are some suggestions for when you are in the car or anywhere else that you and your child have the freedom to raise your voices:

- Go through your child's repertoire of familiar songs with her, and add hand movements and other dramatic improvisations.

- Teach her new songs and sing them together. This is especially fun if you are traveling for a holiday and you can introduce new songs related to the festivities.

- If your child is older, try singing rounds. Two of the most familiar rounds are "Row, Row, Row Your Boat" and "Frere Jacques." You may know others, especially if you were a Scout or attended summer camps when you were a child.

- Create games around songs. Your child can sing a song, substituting "la-la-la" for the words, and you (or another child) has to guess the song from the tune and rhythm. Or, the grown-up sings a song and leaves out a word that the child has to supply, such as, "Old MacDonald had a _____."

- In the car, play cassette tapes or CDs of children's songs, using the car's stereo system or a player that you bring along. See the appendix for suggestions.

Partner Drawing

- **pad of paper**
- **colored markers or crayons**

In this game, you and your child draw a person or thing together. The adult starts by drawing one part, and then the child takes a turn. For example, agree that you are going to draw a face. You draw a round circle, the child then puts in eyes, you add the nose, he adds the mouth, and so on. Let the child be as creative as he likes in this process.

Imaginary Places

This is a good game for encouraging both imagination and visual recall. Start by saying, "Make believe I'm in the grocery store. Here is what I see." Name the objects, or describe everything about the scene. Then say to your child, "Now you make believe you're at the beach (or at a party, at the zoo, in a submarine, in your bedroom, at Uncle Jim's house, at the park). What do you see?" If she has trouble, encourage her with a prompt or two.

OUTINGS

Going to the store, the post office, the bank, and other places about town are often interesting for their own sake. Such excursions can provide a welcome change of scenery, and are especially entertaining if you involve your child in what you are doing. At the grocery store, for example, talk to your child about the choices you are making, what you need to get, the logistics of the store, and the people who work there. At the post office, describe what you are doing and let your child put letters in the slot or hand them to the clerk, check out the scales, and apply stamps. Young children love to learn how to do things, so involving them in the details of your errands is an easy and natural way to keep their spirits up. However, you may find yourself waiting in lines, or your child may be out-of-sorts, or the bustle or unfamiliarity may be frightening, in which case you'll need to go that extra mile. At such times, make-believe games can be very useful.

At the Supermarket

If your three-year-old still fits in the seat of the cart, have him sit there and be a train conductor. An older child can walk next to you as he makes believe he is in charge of a train. Have your child start the engine, and away you go down the aisles. Make sound effects (steam, chugging, the toot-toot or choo-choo of the whistle). Let him know that you need to stop at each "city" to load your supplies into the train. If he's tall enough, he can help collect items.

The more you enter into the spirit of the game, the more fun and effective it will be. Also, lots of praise for being a good train worker will help keep the game going. Be inventive: The frozen foods area can be the North Pole; the produce section can be the jungle; watch out for wild animals or other trains (shopping carts). Chinese food gets us to China; pasta finds us in Italy. The check-out is the last stop, where your conductor can unload the train with you.

At the Department Store

YOU WILL NEED:

- **stroller, for younger children**
- **tote bag or shopping bag**

You can do a number of things to make time in a department store or shopping mall interesting for your child. With two- and three-year-olds, take along a stroller, which can be a cargo truck "driven" by your child. The wide aisles of the mall are highways, and the narrow aisles in the stores are town streets. Have a running conversation about where you are going, and the sights you are passing along the way. This game works whether your child is riding in the stroller or helping to push.

Provide your child with a small tote bag so that he can pretend to be a shopper with you. Let him carry small packages in it, and use his imagination as to what he is shopping for.

Be on the lookout for opportunities to play make-believe games. The escalator can be magic stairs or a mountain, the perfume counter can be a field of flowers, the children's clothing department can be a closet for the biggest family in the world whose imaginary members you can make a game of describing.

Try to shop early, when the store is least crowded, so that you can be in and out as quickly as possible. Also, bringing along something to drink and simple snacks, such as raisins, carrots, and celery, can be a big help if you are out longer than you anticipated.

At the Bank

YOU WILL NEED:

- **coins**
- **coin wrappers**

When you have to go to the bank, have your child pretend that she is a business person. Suggest that she bring pennies, and help her wrap them in a penny wrapper before you go. She can give them to the teller for her own bank deposit or to exchange for larger coins and bills. Both of you can use your imaginations about what sort of work she does to earn her money, and what she plans to do with her wealth. Along with the toys and candy that she might imagine purchasing, suggest acts of charity and philanthropy to help her think about others and the important things she could do to help make the world a better place.

By interacting with the teller and getting to do what she has seen you do, your child will probably be eager to go and well behaved once you're there. Her own receipt or money envelope will make her feel important, and she is likely to be more patient about your errands.

CHALLENGES AT HOME

Unusual experiences are not just the stuff of the outside world. Extraordinary things—such as birthday parties at one end of the spectrum, and staying in bed with the flu at the other—can happen at home as well. Even the most ordinary day is filled with special times at home: meal time, nap time, bath time, bed time. For a young child, these times define the day, adding both structure and interest. Any of these events are prime settings for the normal struggles, stresses, and fears that are part of every child's developmental journey. As such, a repertoire of imaginative games for use during them can help the child develop a generally positive outlook in the face of stress, save face and become cooperative during power struggles, and learn a wealth of coping skills.

Meals

Meal time can sometimes be a contentious or strained experience for children, especially if they are picky eaters. As a general principle, start with very small portions if your child is fussy, because they tend to look more appetizing. The important thing is to keep eating times as stress-free and relaxed as possible, and to try not to be concerned about occasional eating problems. Remember that the child who refuses to eat at one meal will, if not given special treats, be far less picky at the next meal and get what he needs. You can relieve the occasional difficult feeding time with make-believe games, although you should not allow this to develop into a ritual.

DINING COMPANION

Suggest that your child bring a favorite doll or stuffed animal to the table. Have him make a seat for his friend and set a place at the table. He can also put a bib on the companion. When the meal is served, ask your child, "Would Teddy like some chicken?" or "Shall we see if Teddy likes peas?" Place a small amount of each food on the companion's plate. Allowing your child to participate in giving the food to someone else will help him feel that he is in control, and he is likely to be much more cooperative. If the family gets into the spirit of the game and includes your child's guest in conversation, the meal should be a pleasurable event for everyone.

WHAT DO BIRDS EAT?

Your child can make believe that she is a bird, a monkey, a dog, or any other creature she imagines. The more playful you are, the more this game is likely to succeed in lifting your child's spirits and filling her belly. Start by asking her, "What does a bird eat?" Let her come up with some answers, and suggest a few yourself. Try to pick an animal whose diet might bear some physical resemblance, in terms of shape or texture, to your meal. For example, you might be having spaghetti while birds are eating worms; when monkeys are eating grubs you might be serving peas and corn; and on a casserole night your child can pretend she is a dog. Once you have talked about the animal's diet, you might say something like, "Oh, I see some worms on my plate. I am a robin and I love worms! Mmmmm! Look at all these worms!" She is likely to join in the game and take a few bites of her own.

Enhance the game by making sounds like the animal—chirping, soft barking—or imitating it in other ways. However, avoid allowing your child to eat like an animal—that is, gobbling or nibbling directly off of her plate. Sacrificing basic table manners to get a few mouthfuls of food into your child is not necessary or worth the price. When she is hungry enough, she will eat. Meanwhile, consistent rules at the table are important to children's sense of security, as well as their education in social graces.

TELL ME A STORY

A make-believe story at meal time is often relaxing. Sometimes a child becomes so engrossed in the story—especially if you act out all the voices and sounds—that he doesn't even realize he's eating.

In addition to helping with the immediate eating problem, telling stories gives children ideas for their later make-believe play. Moreover, it is a great way to get the family into the habit of being together, talking, and enjoying one another's company during meals. As your child gets older, this can evolve into the casual conversation about the day's events that helps cement healthy families together and gives parents a natural opportunity for keeping up with their children's thoughts and experiences.

The Bath

YOU WILL NEED:

- **bath toys**
- **plastic doll**
- **cups and containers**

Most children love taking baths, but occasionally soap in the eyes or water that's too hot or too cold can turn them against it. But it is difficult to feel frightened while laughing! If your child has become skittish, aim simply for getting him back to enjoying the tub experience, and never mind soap for a bath or two. Coax him into the water with any of these make-believe games:

- Floating toys such as little boats, fish, ducks, and other water animals can make bath time more enjoyable. Get the game going by introducing a scene, then let your child run with it. For example, you might tell your child that the boats are all lined up at the dock, waiting to set sail to catch sight of a magnificent whale or legendary sea creature known to be in nearby waters.

- Washing a doll, including its hair, shows the child that this activity is fun.

- Go fishing. Try to catch a plastic or rubber fish using a net, a kitchen strainer, or a toy fishing pole with a big plastic hook.

- Create weather and geologic patterns in the tub. Whip up a storm. Make waterfalls with cups and buckets. Have your child see if he can make the water as calm and still as possible. Tell stories, and encourage your child to take over the direction of the narrative.

- Sing water songs such as "Row, Row, Row Your Boat" while playing with boats and other water toys.

Bedtime

Some children feel lonely or frightened when put to bed at night or for an afternoon nap. They may need a night light, a special toy in their bed, a sip of water, a story, or a kiss before they go to sleep. This is normal behavior, and as children grow they eventually relinquish such nighttime props. Some children take longer than others to accept bedtime as a routine part of life, however, and they may need some help. Try any of the following bedtime activities that are enhanced with make-believe elements:

- Make up a continuing story that has a new chapter with each nap or bedtime. Children are delighted when stories include references to themselves, their friends, pets, and family members, places they have been, and things they like to do.

- Sing a favorite song to your child, or sing one together. Use soft hand gestures to enact a song. For example, with "Twinkle, Twinkle, Little Star" gently open and close the fingers on your hands to mimic twinkling stars.

- Tell your child to imagine a happy thing and think about it before going to sleep. Suggest a trip to the zoo, a favorite playmate, or playing in the sandbox at the park. These are concrete experiences that children can relive in their mind's eye, relaxing them so that they fall asleep.

- Tell or read a simple storybook of your child's choice, using different voices to dramatize various characters. Most children like to hear the same story many times. Although you can gently suggest new stories, go along willingly if they want the familiar tale they know and love so well.

- Play soothing instrumental music or relaxing nature recordings. Suggest pleasing images and stories to your child as you listen—sitting in cool grass, watching a bird fly—drawing on as many senses as you can.

Try not to prolong this transition period to bed, or you will find yourself involved in an hour-long ritual. Pick one or two bedtime activities and tell your child in advance what you'll be doing together, give yourself enough time to accomplish the activities, and then stick with your plans.

Sick in Bed

When your child is ill, sleep and rest are the main things she needs—and probably wants—while she is feeling her worst. During the recovery period, though, she is lively enough to require diversion even as she must stay in bed. In addition to puzzles, books, and various arts and crafts for the bedridden child, there are plenty of satisfying make-believe games that can be played in bed.

Many of the pretend games described elsewhere in this book can be modified for the sickroom, especially with the help of a bed tray. A bed tray is handy because the hard surface enables the child to play with toys without their falling over or getting lost in the blankets. With "pirates," for example, your child can make an ocean on a tray out of blue crepe paper or construction paper, and assemble characters, boats, an island, fish, and treasure from miniature toys, knick-knacks, and play dough creations. Or, a sick child often likes to play "doctor," and can play this with your assistance while in bed, adapting the ideas from chapter 7, "Roles to Play By," and using dolls or stuffed animals as the patients. And finally, many of the activities described in "Games Worth Waiting For" in this chapter are perfectly suited for the sickroom.

When children are sick, they often become more helpless than usual and more dependent on you. They will probably want their favorite stories read and reread. They will also want you to be near them much of the time, participating in the games they are playing. If an illness necessitates a hospital stay, you can prepare a child by reading books about

going to the hospital, as listed in the appendix. For both home and in the hospital, here are some additional make-believe games to engage the imagination of the recovering child:

YOU WILL NEED:

- **bed tray**
- **miniature people and animal figures**
- **markers or crayons**
- **construction paper**
- **pipe cleaners**
- **play dough**
- **small blocks**
- **small boxes**
- **scrap fabric**
- **puppets**

CIRCUS

A pretend game of circus will always cheer up a sick child. The circus rings can be small loops from a ring toss game or embroidery hoops if you have them. If none of these is available, fashion rings out of pipe cleaners. You need miniature animals, a master of ceremonies, clowns, trapeze artists, animal trainers, and a tightrope walker. Make the people out of play dough or pipe cleaners, or use an assortment of miniature figures. Signs and decorations can be fashioned from construction paper, and markers can be used for the lettering and drawings. For the tightrope, suspend a plastic straw across two stacks of blocks placed several inches apart; anchor the straw in place with pieces of play dough or clay. A trapeze can be a cut-open rubber band, each end anchored with play dough to its own block tower. The actual creation of the circus is a big part of the game!

MUSIC AND MAKE-BELIEVE

Set up a CD or cassette player by the bed while your child is recovering. In the appendix we list songs that allow you and your child to play make-believe games. You may also want to use a radio, trying to find programs that have music for children. If you use tapes or CDs, you and your child can sing along, and follow suggestions for simple hand movements or voice sound effects such as a squeaky door, a car skidding, machine noises, or animal sounds.

PUPPET SHOW

A sickbed puppet show can be a source of amusement for your youngster, and for other members of the family, who can be the audience. A small carton or a shoe box set on its side and placed on a bed tray serves as a fine theater or stage. Favorite fairy tales or nursery rhymes can offer story lines. Encourage your child to make up stories, too, and to use different voices. Use hand or finger puppets. Make people and animals out of play dough or pipe cleaners. Help construct simple props out of paper, blocks, and small plastic containers. Little trees or bushes can be made out of play dough. Build tables and chairs for the puppets out of small blocks and boxes. Pieces of scrap fabric can be curtains, tablecloths, and costumes. Again, the fun of making the puppets and scenery is a major part of the game and helps the time go by quickly.

READ-ALOUD MAKE-BELIEVE

Read to your youngster often when he is ill. If you both act out parts and take on the voices of characters, you will find that reading together offers a great deal of mutual pleasure. Books are listed in the appendix according to topics. You might want to choose your stories so that they coincide with the games you play on a given day, such as a circus story to go with a circus game. Select stories that are funny or soothing, and steer away from those that are sad or scary.

You can't be with your child every moment. During times when your child is by herself, provide her with stories on tape. Most public libraries have a good selection of books on tape for children.

GRAB BAG

Guessing games are fun for most children, even when they are sick. Put several items (wooden block, feather, shoelace, spoon, button, etc.) into a bag or pillowcase, and have the child reach into the bag, grab an item, and try to identify it without looking at it.

Birthday Parties

To be honest, many parents have come to dread both giving and attending birthday parties for toddlers and preschoolers. However, by keeping a few points in mind, parties for young children can be occasions for pure fun and celebration. The secrets of a successful party for preschool children are:

- Keep it small. A good rule of thumb is to invite approximately as many children as your child's age in years.

- Limit the time to an hour, or an hour and a half at the most, and be sure your invitation specifies the ending time. A one-hour party allows time for greetings, a game or two, ice cream and cake, opening of presents, and goodbyes, before the excitement and the goodies send the children out of control. For two- and three-year-olds, ask the parents to stay during the party, and have refreshments on hand for them as well as the children.

- Give each guest a simple party favor to take home. Parties generate excitement and tension to begin with, and the visiting children are inevitably envious of the birthday child. Favors may reduce jealousy over the gifts received by the birthday child. They may consist of colorful bags filled with miniature toys and snacks, such as a small box of raisins, a granola bar, dried fruit, or candies.

- Consider requesting that guests not bring gifts. You can avoid much of the jealousy, and focus on the non-material joys of celebration.

- Include the birthday child in the planning and preparation. Let her choose the theme, colors for paper goods and candles, the hats, and the favors (but keep the cake a surprise!), and do as much preparation as possible before the actual day of the party.

- Avoid competitive party games for preschoolers, because children at this age are often broken-hearted when they lose. Instead, try any of the following imaginative games:

YOU WILL NEED:

- **construction paper**
- **tape**
- **glue sticks**
- **assorted decorations**

PARTY HAT

A good way to get the party going is to have everyone make a hat. Fill a large box with plenty of odds and ends—buttons, strips of crepe paper, ribbons, yarn, scraps of fabric, pipe cleaners, colored feathers, and so on. Give everyone a basic cone-style hat that is made from construction paper and taped together. Also, give each child a glue stick. Have all of the guests select items from the box to decorate their hat. Supervise the activity, and assist as needed. Encourage the children to wear their hats and to invent stories about who they are, as represented by their hats.

ROUND STORY

Gather the children in a circle on the floor, and begin to tell a story. Ask each child in turn to add some event to it. This works well with four- and five-year-olds. If possible, make an audio recording of it, and play it back for the children. You might consider making copies of the tape for each guest as a memento.

RHYTHM AND DANCE

If you play music CDs or tapes, such as those listed in the appendix, the children can dance or move to the music as the song suggests. Children enjoy music and dancing, plus the activity allows them to let off some steam.

GUESS WHAT!

Fill a big bag or pillowcase with distinctive objects in terms of shape or texture, and let each child close her eyes, reach in, and feel an item. She says what it is—without peeking!—and then pulls it out. (Keep the item out of the bag.) Have more items in the bag than there are children to play.

PUPPET PARTY

Use a large puppet stage, such as the one described in chapter 6, "Poems, Songs, and Stories," and help the children put on a simple play called "Birthday Party." Each child has a puppet on her hand and comes to the party on the stage, one by one. A small cupcake with unlit candles can be the birthday cake, and everyone can sing "Happy Birthday to You." For a variation, play "Happy Un-Birthday," singing "Happy Un-Birthday to You" and listing all of the guests' names in the song.

PARTY PIRATES

In yet another adaptation of "pirates," give each child a scarf to wear on his head, or some other item of pirate garb, and assemble the children in an area that you have specially prepared to be the pirates'

"cave." Tell the group a story about shipwreck and buried treasure. In the story, the captain tells the pirate crew that the island they have sailed to has enough treasure for everyone, and that each of the pirates will have their own day to hunt for treasure. Be the voice of the captain and call out, "It's Monday, and it's Pirate Jake's crack at huntin' fer treasure. The rest of ye merry pirates shall cheer 'im on!"

Have inexpensive favors hidden in easy places around the room, and allow the children one by one to search for them. Whisper "hot," "warm," or "cold," as appropriate, to the other pirates, who call out this information to the seeker to indicate how close the child is to finding a piece of treasure. Allow each child to have a turn and to find something. After Jake has found a favor, for example, he returns to the pirate cave, and you say, "Now it's Tuesday, and it's time for Pirate Sasha to go a-huntin'!" Continue until all of the children have had their turn.

CHAPTER TEN

Using Television For Imaginative Growth

In most homes in the United States, television is virtually a member of the family. The average American child grows up reacting not only to the words, facial expressions, and movements of real people around her but also to those of the little characters who move across the screen in the living room, family room, or den. Television is a powerful influence on growing children and on our culture, imparting a vast array of information and emotional material.

Imagine through a child's eyes: On one channel she sees a group of swirling dancers in an old musical; on another, a baseball game in which men throw balls and hit them with a stick; on a third, grown-ups whom everyone laughs at; on a fourth, scenes of people in a strange jungle-like land beating drums, jumping up and down with spears and shields, and wearing very little clothing. Action is fast, and

scenes move quickly. Days, months, and even years are telescoped into time frames of 30 or 60 minutes. Special camera tricks make people move in slow motion, appear to climb buildings, fly through the air, and run backwards. Zoom effects make people and things seem larger than they are. In cartoons, characters are squashed, mashed, and pulled apart, only to reappear whole again.

What is a child to make of this? How do the diverse people, actions, and places become a part of the day-to-day imagination of the child? Is there a way to help children sort it all out? Parents wonder, does television help their children...or does it harm them?

A few parents simply ban it from their homes. Indeed, children reared without television tend to develop flexible imaginations and scarcely seem to miss the set at all. But most people are not prepared to go this far. Besides the fact that youngsters enjoy television, including educational programs, many parents also believe that their children learn from television such things as new words, facts about the world, and ways to behave.

However, television alone may not be the teacher that some think it is. Yes, if a parent uses it to explain ideas or to help a child distinguish between what is real and what is not real, television can be a rich source of information. Without such help from an adult, though, TV can take an unhealthy control of the child and lead to heavy viewing without much understanding.

THE BAD NEWS: NEGATIVE EFFECTS OF TELEVISION ON CHILDREN

More than 98 percent of American homes have television sets, and these sets are turned on for an average of more than seven hours a day. Since the 1960s, behavioral scientists have been researching how the life-altering phenomenon of TV affects growing children. Results indicate that when television is not used with care, it can have a negative impact on social skills, emotional well-being, and cognitive development. For specific documentation of the effects of television described below, see *The Handbook of Children and the Media,* edited by ourselves, and other sources listed in the bibliography section in the back of this book.

Social Skills and Aggression
Many parents and citizens' groups such as the Center for Media

Education in Washington, DC, and a former advocacy organization called Action for Children's Television have called attention to the possibility that children become aggressive as a result of the violence they witness on television. This concern is justified.

We find, from our research and from the research of many others, that some children who are heavy viewers—watching four or more hours a day—have more trouble playing with other children in a positive, constructive way. They are more bossy and angry, and do not share or cooperate well. They hit and push other children, and destroy toys and property. They may get into trouble in school at an early age. The most aggressive of these children typically watch action shows and cartoons, which have extremely high rates of violence, but see little or no educational TV, such as *Barney & Friends, Mister Rogers' Neighborhood,* or *Sesame Street.* They also have little in their lives other than TV to help them develop an ability to get along with other children or to develop learning skills needed in school. For example, they rarely visit a zoo, library, or museum, or they eat dinner with the TV on and stay up late watching it.

A number of careful research studies have demonstrated that young children, especially those who already hit others, behave more aggressively than they otherwise do after viewing shows with violent scenes, even simple-minded cartoons such as *Batman.* One important study carried out over a period of 20 years in upstate New York demonstrated that the amount of violence exhibited by young adults by the time they were 18 to 20 years old, and later 20 to 30, could be best explained (among all other factors studied) by the amount of television violence they had viewed as children. And in numerous experiments conducted over the past 30 years, the results consistently concluded that children imitate aggressive acts that they witness.

Anxiety

Teenagers and adults are often attracted to suspense and danger in television and movies. They allow themselves to be carried to the brink of fear and then back off from it, possessing the wisdom to know that monsters do not exist, that the show is not reality. But young children don't have the experience or the thinking capacity to deal with suspense shows. While they may be initially fascinated, their subsequent reaction can easily be one of terror. Nightmares, night terrors, and fear of the dark in young children are often the result of such viewing.

When young children go to sleep at night, they have no intellectual or cognitive structures to reassure them about the darkness and the strange play of shadows and lights across the room. The temptation is to attribute such phenomena to mysterious or supernatural forces, bogey men, goblins, or monsters. Add to these any of the sinister characters vividly portrayed on television, and one can see how easily the imagination of the child can be led down frightening paths. Programs that have deliberately developed suspense and terror as part of their format are very disturbing to them.

Cognitive Development and Learning

Heavy television viewing, regardless of content, has an undesirable effect on a child's ability to learn in a number of ways. First, it increases restlessness and leads to difficulty in concentration. Children who spend more than four hours a day watching TV typically cannot stay with a game or with a puzzle for more than a few minutes. It may be that the constant change of scenes on television hinders their ability to stick with one activity.

Second, contrary to many parents' expectations, research indicates that heavy television viewers are not developing their vocabulary as well as light television viewers. In order to learn new words, children need to practice saying what they hear. We find that children who play make-believe games and who seldom watch television use more words and more parts of speech than children who do not play imaginatively and who do watch a lot of television. When children play make-believe games, they need to employ language in order to keep the game going. Think of all the words a child needs to play "pirate": ship, wind, sail, island, shovel, dig, sand, gold, rubies, eye-patch, treasure, map, and so on. Children learn best when they say words out loud and when they use them in games—when they are actively doing things rather than watching from the sidelines.

Third, television can interfere with learning how to read. Some scientific research has found that when a TV set was introduced into homes, reading skills were acquired more slowly by the children in those homes than by those who did not yet have television. We have found in our studies at Yale University that elementary school-age children who watch a lot of television have significantly lower reading scores than children who don't watch as much.

Finally, heavy television viewing can make a child less rather than more interested in the world. If he sits motionless for long periods of time taking in a stream of programming, a child can become more passive, rather than more eager or more curious or more imaginative. The vast amount of material that such a child absorbs is not sorted out properly, and much of it is confusing, so that effective learning may not occur.

THE GOOD NEWS: THE CONSTRUCTIVE POTENTIAL OF TELEVISION

And yet, despite these risks, television has the potential to do a lot of good. In measured doses, for example, it can stimulate the imagination, in that many of the make-believe games that children play can use characters, themes, scenes, and plots suggested by television. In our own research we have observed that three- and four-year-olds are more imaginative and joyful after watching a program such as *Mister Rogers' Neighborhood*, particularly when an adult has been sitting with them during viewing.

Children have also been shown to behave in a more helpful, friendly, and cooperative manner after watching such programs. Depending on the nature and source of programming, children can and do absorb positive social values from TV.

In terms of learning, studies have shown that children acquire both reading readiness and number skills from educational programs such as *Sesame Street* and *Barney & Friends*. Also, well-chosen shows of high quality can introduce useful information about geography, cultural mythology, and history. As American psychologist Robert Liebert has put it, television truly has the potential to open "a window on the world."

In short, television can be stimulating and helpful for children's development in several important ways, as long as certain fundamental considerations are met: One, the right programs have to be selected, and two, the amount of time spent viewing TV must be limited. When adults watch with their children and talk about the content of the shows, the benefits appear to be even greater.

SETTING THE RULES

Children make the best use of television when their parents create and stick with a fairly firm set of rules about viewing times, circumstances, and kinds of programs. Viewing times can mean both time of day and the amount of time spent watching TV. Circumstances might include watching only with a parent, and watching before or after some other event, such as getting dressed or, for older children, doing homework or chores. And of course, program rules have to do with the content of the show itself. Therefore, your three-year-old might

be permitted to watch either *Mister Rogers' Neighborhood* or *Barney & Friends*, which are 30 minutes each, on weekday mornings with you, a grandparent, or perhaps a daycare provider. Many parents find that a chart listing the shows that a child may watch, along with their times, is easy to follow and helps eliminate discussion, bargaining, and confusion.

Parents have the easiest time managing healthy viewing policies when they are implemented from the very beginning. Sometime between the ages of 12 and 18 months, children become increasingly aware of the television set and start to react to it. A child at this age may not pause in front of the set for long and certainly will have difficulty comprehending what is going on. Still, parents may now consider initiating the child into a TV orientation that will keep viewing under control and minimize its dangers. This may mean thinking through the whole household's viewing patterns. In families with young children, the television should be turned on only if somebody is actively watching. Also, if older children watch TV, parents are advised to monitor their shows while a much younger child is around. Other guidelines would include making sure that your child is not using television to take the place of other active or social or educational experiences, and only permitting television after the child has spent some time in other activities, including both reading and energetic play with brothers, sisters, or friends.

When a child is 24 months old, one parent might get into a regular habit of watching a specific show with her. Choose a program that is carefully geared toward very young children, with a set time, so that a definite pattern of viewing can be established. When viewing is this structured and predictable, children don't expect free access to the television, nor do they come to think of TV as something to do when nothing else comes to mind. If children know from the start that there are firm limits, they accept those limits as a natural part of their daily life.

TIME LIMITS Even with the best programming, there can be too much of a good thing. When a child is watching television, she is not playing, being physically active, socializing, and otherwise going about the important business of being a child. Therefore, we recommend setting limits on the amount of time that children spend in front of the set.

For the youngest child, a maximum of 30 minutes a day is plenty, if she lasts even that long. Two-year-olds may not pay more than intermittent attention to a television show, and even a three- or four-year-old may not stay put until the end. If she begins to roam around the room or wants to do something else, by all means don't force her to pay attention.

Three- and young four-year-olds should watch no more than one hour a day. Older preschoolers can watch up to two hours a day, preferably not in one sitting, if the programs are geared for their age group and have some educational value.

CHOOSING THE RIGHT PROGRAM

Shows for Two- and Three-Year-Olds
The best shows for toddlers have a positive attitude. They tailor their vocabulary to the very young, include humor and novelty, have recur-

ring central characters who are likable, and avoid frightening scenes. Parents and teachers of two- and three-year-olds should look for programs with these features:

- A central adult figure, male or female, conveys a sense of personal interest and concern to your child. This central figure is portrayed as warm, stable, and effective.

- The pace is slow enough so that children can savor the show.

- The show provides sufficient entertainment value in the form of story material, opportunities to laugh, or demonstrations of interesting sights or objects.

- There are no truly frightening or dangerous scenes, or indications of punishment to children or animals.

- The program inspires imaginative play, featuring, for example, characters that the child may want to imitate.

- The distinction between reality and fantasy is made very clear.

Children love fantasy characters and make-believe elements, but their first viewing experiences should keep reality and fantasy completely separate, so that they can begin to learn the difference. For this reason, most cartoon shows are not recommended. On the other hand, fantasy material is fine when it is introduced by a central adult figure on a TV show. For example, in *Mister Rogers' Neighborhood*, Mr. Rogers carefully explains to children what is real and what is not real, and transitions to the fantasy world in ways that are very clear to the child, much as a parent or teacher might say, "Now I am going to tell you a story." In this way, children get the fun of the fantasy while learning the crucial distinction between fantasy and reality.

Shows for Older Preschoolers

Once children are past the age of two-and-a-half or three, parents and teachers may experiment with a greater variety of shows. Youngsters continue to enjoy such programs as *Mister Rogers' Neighborhood*,

Noddy, Sesame Street, and *Barney & Friends* through the ages of four and five, but they are ready for more complex programs, such as *Wishbone, Franklin, Arthur,* and *The Magic School Bus.* In addition to weekday educational programs such as *Sesame Street,* you may try expanding your child's viewing to some Saturday morning shows. In recent years, the major networks have improved this programming so that it better reflects the importance of positive social experience and altruistic or socially helpful behavior. They have also reduced the level of violence. Parents should preview potential new shows and look for the following:

- Programs that tell well-known stories clearly and without adult "show-biz" cynicism are desirable. Fairy tales of the less frightening kind, ancient myths, and adventures from history are all much appreciated by four- and five-year-olds.

- Realistic animal stories are sources of great delight. Children begin to develop important feelings of love and warmth, as well as a sense of caretaking, when watching accounts of how animals are treated with love by other children. Ample opportunities for minor misadventure and mishap add just enough tension to be interesting but not frightening.

- Fairly realistic cartoons that involve stories of small groups of children who band together (whether in a family or as friends) to deal with adventurous circumstances, to build or construct things, or to help other children, adults, or animals not only entertain preschoolers but also point the way to constructive make-believe play situations.

- Stylish programs that introduce children to new art forms—music, dance, puppetry—can be extremely stimulating and evoke lots of imaginative play.

- Some family situation comedies are suitable, when watched with parents or the family. It's important that the adults point out the similarities and differences between the show and the child's own family. Also, parents need to preview these programs and avoid those that expose children to false values, portrayals of the father as a bumbler or the mother as a shrew, or an emphasis on well-to-do surroundings or unusually talented children.

Shows to Avoid

Be on guard against any of the following when selecting programs for children between the ages two and five:

- portrayals of great danger or threat to animals, children, or parent figures;
- excessive spookiness and unexplained supernatural characters, such as monsters engaged in scary activities;
- violence or physical attack in realistic or familiar settings;
- cartoons or fantasy programs that show dismemberment, physical wounds, mutilation, or violent physical contact;
- risky athletic or physical activities.

Violence can be terrifying for preschoolers and lead to nightmares, frightening fantasies, and general anxiety, especially when it involves dismemberment or other extreme harm to parent figures, children, and other vulnerable creatures. Scenes of violence can also lead to imitation, especially when the setting is familiar to the child, or involves children, pets, or family members. Violence in very remote settings—such as the highly stylized fighting that takes place in historical movies or far-flung cultures—is less likely to encourage imitation but should still be avoided. Even fantasy shows that pit superheros against evil may be remembered not for their be-good message but rather their spectacular punches and kicks—which then get imitated on the playground.

Indeed, any activity that spurs imitation but is potentially dangerous to the child or others should be actively avoided. If a child does see a risky physical activity on TV, an adult needs to explain that this is a performance. It is something that a child can imitate only in make-believe ways, with miniature toy cars or objects, for example, but never with his own tricycle. Keep in mind that children will try to imitate just about anything. Even gentle Mr. Rogers, who used to toss his sneaker up in the air and catch it on his program, has modified the ritual because youngsters were following suit and getting bonked on the head!

WATCHING TELEVISION WITH YOUR CHILD

Most of us are familiar with the sight of a child staring glassy-eyed at the television set. But when you speak to him, it's as if you have flipped a switch and turned him on. He comes to life and his mind engages. When grown-ups interact with children while they are watching television, the effect is profound. Viewing becomes an active learning and social experience rather than a passive and potentially numbing one. Your child is able to absorb and understand more information—and misunderstand less—when you talk about the program together. And in the bargain, the two of you get to know each other better and share some precious moments.

When it's time for a program to start, treat the event like a planned activity. You might have special seating such as a favorite chair or pillows to sit on. Your child might bring another friend along, such as a favorite stuffed animal, doll, or the family dog. If it's an educational program that typically includes alphabet and number segments, she might have toy letters and numbers to play with and talk about as you are watching together. Preparing for the show builds excitement, encourages your child to think ahead, and provides more opportunity for interaction.

During the program, sit close together; you might even hold a two-year-old in your lap. The rule of thumb is to point things out and ask questions so that you engage your child in an easygoing dialogue. Children are usually delighted to have grown-ups around saying things like, "Oh, look at that duck Leon is holding. It's a real duck. What does it sound like?" In this way, you can attempt to get the child to interact with both you and the object on the screen, and you can answer questions and explain in simple terms what Leon is doing with the duck.

As you view with your child, keep in mind the following:

• Tell children (especially preschoolers) when something is real and when it is make believe.

• If something is too complicated for the child, try to explain it.

• If a program becomes frightening or too exciting, turn off the set and engage the child in some other interesting toy or game.

• With older children who can handle material that is somewhat frightening, discuss how the material is not real and how the camera and other elements such as music operate to make a scene seem scary.

• Use television as an ice-breaker for conversations about emotions and problems.

• When anger, jealousy, worry, sadness, or joy and happiness are presented in a story plot, point out the situations and talk about how the story is the same or different from what happens in your lives or family.

• Use the material presented on television to teach children about various races, religions, cultures, and nationalities.

• Clear up misunderstandings or early prejudices that might be stimulated by representations of certain characters in a story as wrong, evil, weak, or stupid.

Families can use television as a treat: a special occasion that includes cultural entertainment and an opportunity to share feelings. Such experiences help establish good communication between children and their parents, and create lasting memories. By selecting special

A NOTE ABOUT OTHER ELECTRONIC MEDIA

Families are increasingly using videos, CD-ROMs, and computer software with their preschoolers. It is natural for parents to want to expose their children to these advanced and often more interactive technologies, but the same principles outlined for television viewing should be applied to these materials. Keep in mind the risk of isolating a child before a repetitive game that can be diverting but at the same time may offer little in the way of new information or stimulation for the imagination. In addition, many video games are quite violent, and research indicates that playing such games can have effects similar to those of watching aggressive television. These new forms of entertainment require the same monitoring of content that television programs do.

THE V-CHIP

The content of television programs is now rated for violence (denoted with a "V") and other material that may be inappropriate for children. All new television sets purchased after January 2000 have the "V-chip," which allows you to block out programs that contain objectionable material. See "Resources" on page 175 for information on how to obtain a rating guide.

programs of a high quality, planning the viewing so that all family members can participate, and then enjoying the show as a group, you create an atmosphere that makes for an enriching experience of togetherness that children will treasure now and in the future.

And finally, use television as an active tool for playing and learning after viewing. Wherever possible look for ideas that you can imitate. Get down on the floor with your children and start off a game based on something you've just watched. They will soon take over and move the game in their own direction, as they usually do, and you can phase yourself out. Look for specific activities too. If a character plants seeds, why not you? Active participation in even small projects like this helps children learn far more than simple viewing can teach.

Approached wisely, television can a source for a whole variety of plots and characters, entertainment possibilities, and learning opportunities, feeding the imagination rather than substituting for it. On the following pages we present games and activities to help preschoolers make full use of their television viewing to learn, enjoy, and stretch the mind. §

TELEVISION GAMES

Let's Find It

SIZE IT UP

Explore "big versus small" with your children. Together find something small on a program you are viewing, and then find something big on the program. Afterward, find something small in a room of your home or school, and then something big.

Play a variation and explore the concept "more versus less" by asking the children who has the most things to say or do on the television show. Who has less, or the least?

THINGS THAT GO TOGETHER

Help children learn to classify, an important feature of thinking, by asking, for example, where are all the square things on the program? Find them together. Look for things that are round. Look for things that are on the floor, on the wall, on the ceiling. Match colors: Find red things, find blue things. Match by functions: things that ride, things for drinking, things you wear. Look for animals, and name them. Look for furniture, and identify each piece.

ALPHABET GAME

Have the children look for characters or objects on their favorite television show that begin with a specific letter or sound, such as S or B. They might find Snoopy or Big Bird. Help them get used to listening to sounds of letters, not just the names of letters, which is the first step in learning to read.

Weather Watch

To help children learn about nature and science, watch the weather news together. Talk about different kinds of weather. Keep a chart to see how often the TV predictions are correct. Make paper suns, clouds, raindrops, and snowflakes, and pin those representing both the prediction and the actual weather on the chart each day. Every week or so, count up the results to see how often the weatherperson was right. As your child gets older, you can introduce con-

cepts such as weather patterns and climates, and talk about how clouds, rain, and snow are formed.

TV Tunes

When music is featured during a segment on a program, have the children stand up and move to the beat. Clap hands in rhythm to help get the beat, and talk about fast versus slow music. If the music is played to enhance a story, ask the children how the music makes them feel, and talk about how it affects their feelings about the story or the characters they are watching in the story.

Guess Who I Am?

Ask the child, "Guess who I am?" and make believe you are a character from a program that you watch with him. Describe and act out the character until your child can guess who it is. Suggest he take a turn at being a character. Encourage your child to become more perceptive of the qualities of the person or fantasy figure in the story—friendliness, grouchiness, generosity, and other traits. What emotions is the character showing? Identify some of the physical characteristics of the person, such as size, strength or weakness, and style of clothing. You can help your child build an awareness of appearance and emotional expression, and at the same time build his vocabulary around these concepts.

Getting Along

When a program is over, select a part of the story that was related to how we get along with others, adults or children. Talk about one social idea with your child. For example, if a character on a favorite show shared an object that day, play sharing with your child. Play sharing with dolls or puppets first; later you may see your child sharing her crayons or cookies with her brother. Taking turns and other prosocial skills can be practiced in this way. Also, effective discussions about jealousy, fear, love, and anger can all be stimulated by television stories. *Arthur* and *Franklin* frequently present good stories for such ideas.

Commercial Break

Within minutes of a child's first experience with network television, she will be exposed to the world of commercial advertising. Help your child develop a healthy objectivity toward such advertising by constructively talking about the real advantages and disadvantages of toys, cereals, and other items that are promoted to your child. Also, talk about the fact that the advertiser doesn't really know what you want or need or what is best for you, pointing out that the purpose of commercials is simply to sell an item.

One effective way to introduce consumer education is to make a game of it and have your children make up their own commercials, using actual toys and foods or products of their own invention. Children can act out their commercials themselves or use puppets. You might talk with them in advance about the good points of a product. You might also point out a negative aspect of a product that an advertiser would avoid mentioning, so that your child understands that what is *not* said is important, too. Help with props, background, and costumes.

Parents and teachers may feel they are walking a fine line. You want to encourage an ability to evaluate with open eyes, but not an attitude of cynicism and distrust. At the same time, you don't want your child to learn that a "do what you can get away with" morality is an acceptable credo to live by in the real world. If you sense your child drifting one way or the other, gently guide him in the right direction.

You're on TV!

Make a TV set out of a large cardboard box. Set it on a table that is covered by a cloth. The child can stand behind the table so that his lower body is concealed by the cloth and his upper body appears on the makeshift TV screen. He can wear a simple costume and act out a familiar story. Grown-ups and other children can be the audience. Bravo!

APPENDIX

Recommended Reading and Listening for Children

Books by Topic

ANIMALS AND ANIMALS IN PEOPLE SITUATIONS

Adbjornsen, Peter Christen. *The Three Billy Goats Gruff.* New York: HarperCollins, 1998.
Bridwell, Norman. *Clifford and the Big Storm.* New York: Scholastic, 1995.
Brunhoff, Jean de. *The Story of Babar* (and all sequels). New York: Random House, 1966.
Carle, Eric. *The Very Busy Spider.* New York: Putnam, 1995.
Carlstrom, Nancy W. *Jesse Bear, What Will You Wear?* New York: Simon & Schuster, 1996.
Christelow, Eileen. *Don't Wake Up Mama! Another Five Little Monkeys Story.* Boston: Houghton Mifflin, 1996.
Christelow, Eileen. *Five Little Monkeys Sitting in a Tree.* Boston: Clarion, 1993.
Ember, Kathi. *Old MacDonald Had a Farm.* New York: Western, 1997.
Ginsburg, Mirra. *Across the Stream.* New York: Morrow, 1991.
Hill, Eric. *Spot & Friends Play.* New York: Putnam, 1996.
Keats, Ezra Jack. *Whistle for Willie.* New York: Puffin, 1977.
Martin Jr., Bill. *Brown Bear, Brown Bear, What Do You See?* New York: Holt, 1996.
McCloskey, Robert. *Make Way for Ducklings.* New York: Puffin, 1993.
Numeroff, Laura. *If You Give a Mouse a Cookie.* New York: HarperCollins, 1997.
Numeroff, Laura. *If You Give a Moose a Muffin.* New York: HarperCollins, 1997.
Rey, H.A. *Curious George.* Boston: Houghton Mifflin, 1973.
Seuss, Dr. *One Fish, Two Fish, Red Fish, Blue Fish.* New York: Random House, 1966.
Shaw, Nancy. *Sheep in a Jeep.* Boston: Houghton Mifflin, 1997.
Slobodkina, Esphyr. *Caps for Sale.* New York: Scholastic, 1993.
Steig, William. *Doctor De Soto.* New York: Farrar, Straus & Giroux, 1990.
Useman, Sharon and Ernie. *Tibby Tried It.* Washington, DC: Magination Press, 1999.

BIRTHDAYS AND HOLIDAYS

Brown, Marc. *Arthur's April Fool.* New York: Little Brown, 1985.
Brown, Margaret Wise. *On Christmas Eve.* New York: HarperCollins, 1996.
Bunting, Eve. *Flower Garden.* San Diego: Harcourt, Brace, 1994.
Bunting, Eve. *Happy Birthday, Dear Duck.* Boston: Houghton Mifflin, 1990.
Bunting, Eve. *The Mother's Day Mice.* Boston: Houghton Mifflin, 1986.
Bunting, Eve. *A Perfect Father's Day.* Boston: Houghton Mifflin, 1993.
Hoff, Syd. *Happy Birthday, Danny & the Dinosaur!* New York: HarperCollins, 1995.
Keats, Ezra Jack. *A Letter to Amy.* New York: HarperCollins, 1968.
Rice, Eve. *Benny Bakes a Cake.* New York: Greenwillow, 1993.
Shaw, Nancy. *Sheep in a Shop.* Boston: Houghton Mifflin, 1991.
Wormell, Mary. *Hilda Hen's Happy Birthday.* San Diego, CA: Harcourt, Brace, 1995.

CHANGE AND GROWTH

Birnbaum, A. *Green Eyes.* New York: Western, 1973.
Brinckloe, Julie. *Fireflies!* New York: Macmillan, 1985.
Burton, Virginia Lee. *Mike Mulligan and His Steam Shovel.* Boston: Houghton Mifflin, 1977.
Cain, Barbara. *I Don't Know Why...I Guess I'm Shy.* Washington, DC: Magination Press, 2000.
Climo, Shirley. *Little Red Ant and the Great Big Crumb.* Boston: Houghton Mifflin, 1995.
Goldsmith, Howard. *Shy Little Turtle.* New York: McGraw-Hill, 1998.
Keats, Ezra Jack. *Jennie's Hat.* New York: HarperCollins, 1985.
Keller, Holly. *Geraldine's Blanket.* New York: Greenwillow, 1984.
Moss, Thylias. *I Want to Be.* New York: Dial, 1993.
Silverstein, Shel. *The Giving Tree.* New York: Lectorum Publications, 1996.
Tripp, Paul. *The Little Red Flower.* New York: Doubleday, 1968.

EMOTIONS, SENSES, AND THE BODY

Baker, Alan. *Benjamin's Dreadful Dream.* Philadelphia: Lippincott-Raven, 1980.
Becker, Jim, and Andy Mayer. *Look and Listen Fire Trucks.* New York: Scholastic, 1993.
Becker, Jim, and Andy Mayer. *Look and Listen Work Trucks.* New York: Scholastic, 1993.
Berger, Melvin. *All About Sound.* New York: Scholastic, 1994.
Cain, Barbara. *Double-Dip Feelings: Stories to Help Children Understand Emotions.* Washington, DC: Magination Press, 1990.
Carle, Eric. *The Grouchy Ladybug.* New York: HarperCollins, 1996.
Carter, Noelle. *Where's My Squishy Ball?* New York: Scholastic, 1993.
Cole, Joanna. *The Magic School Bus Explores the Senses.* New York: Scholastic, 1999.
Freeman, Don. *Corduroy.* New York: Puffin, 1993.
Hoban, Tana. *Is It Rough, Is It Smooth, Is It Shiny?* New York: Greenwillow, 1984.
Huth, Holly Y. *Darkfright.* New York: Simon & Schuster, 1996.
Joosse, Barbara. *Mama, Do You Love Me?* San Francisco: Chronicle Books, 1991.
Leghorn, Lindsey. *Proud of Our Feelings.* Washington, DC: Magination Press, 1995.
Lillie, Patricia. *Floppy Teddy Bear.* New York: Greenwillow, 1995.
Martin, C.L. *Three Brave Women.* New York: Simon & Schuster, 1991.
Mayer, Gina, & Mercer Mayer. *A Very Special Critter.* New York: Western, 1993.
Miller, Margaret. *My Five Senses.* New York: Simon & Schuster, 1994.
Perkins, Al. *Hand, Hand, Fingers, Thumb.* New York: Random House, 1998.
Strub, Susanne. *My Dog, My Sister and I.* New York: Morrow, 1993.
Tafuri, Nancy. *The Brass Ring.* New York: Greenwillow, 1996.
Yurcheshen, Richard. *My Gum Is Gone.* Washington, DC: Magination Press, 2000.
Zolotow, Charlotte. *The Hating Book.* New York: HarperCollins, 1989.

EVERYDAY LIFE EVENTS

Ackerman, Karen. *This Old House.* New York: Macmillan, 1992.
Baker, Jeannie. *Window.* New York: Greenwillow, 1991.
Brown, Margaret Wise. *Goodnight Moon.* New York: HarperCollins, 1989.
Cooper, Elisha. *Country Fair.* New York: Greenwillow, 1997.

Hayes, Sarah. *Eat Up, Gemma.* New York: Lothrop, Lee & Shepard, 1988.
Hoban, Russell. *A Bargain for Frances.* New York: HarperCollins, 1992.
Johnson, Angela. *The Leaving Morning.* New York: Orchard, 1992.
Krauss, Ruth. *A Hole Is to Dig.* New York: HarperCollins, 1989.
Lillie, Patricia. *Everything Has a Place.* New York: Greenwillow, 1993.
Morris, Ann. *Hats, Hats, Hats.* New York: Morrow, 1993.
Rasmussen, Ann, and Marc Nemiroff. *The Very Lonely Bathtub.* Washington, DC: Magination Press, 2000.
Rockwell, Anne. *Show and Tell Day.* New York: HarperCollins, 1997.

FAMILY RELATIONS

Cooper, Helen. *Little Monster Did It!* New York: Dial, 1996.
Doro, Ann. *Twin Pickle.* New York: Holt, 1996.
Fluornoy, Valerie. *The Patchwork Quilt.* New York: Dial, 1985.
Gackenbach, Dick. *Where Are Momma, Poppa, and Sister June?* Boston: Houghton Mifflin, 1994.
Hausherr, Rosemarie. *Celebrating Families.* New York: Scholastic, 1997.
Hoban, Russell. *A Baby Sister for Frances.* New York: HarperCollins, 1976.
Hoban, Russell. *Bread and Jam for Frances.* New York: HarperCollins, 1993.
Hutchins, Pat. *The Doorbell Rang.* New York: Greenwillow, 1986.
Johnson, Dolores. *What Will Mommy Do When I'm at School?* New York: Aladdin Paperbacks, 1988.
Keats, Ezra Jack. *Apartment Three.* New York: Simon & Schuster, 1986.
Keats, Ezra Jack. *Peter's Chair.* New York: HarperCollins, 1983.
Lowell, Gloria Roth. *Elana's Ears, or How I Became the Best Big Sister in the World.* Washington, DC: Magination Press, 2000.
Mayer, Mercer. *Just Me and My Little Sister.* New York: Western, 1986.
Pelham, David. *Sam's Pizza.* New York: Dutton, 1996.
Wild, Margaret. *Our Granny.* Boston: Houghton Mifflin, 1998.

FANTASY AND NURSERY RHYMES

Ahlberg, Janet and Allan. *Each Peach Pear Plum.* New York: Puffin, 1986.
Aylesworth, Jim. *Gingerbread Man.* New York: Scholastic, 1998.
Balducci, Rita. *Jack and the Beanstalk.* New York: Western, 1994.
Barton, Byron. *The Little Red Hen.* New York: HarperCollins, 1993.
Desimini, Lisa. *Moon Soup.* New York: Hyperion, 1993.
Galdone, Paul. *Little Red Riding Hood.* New York: McGraw-Hill, 1974.
Galdone, Paul. *Rumpelstiltskin.* Boston: Houghton Mifflin, 1985.
Galdone, Paul. *The Three Bears.* Boston: Houghton Mifflin, 1979.
Greenway, Jennifer. *Three Little Pigs.* Kansas City: Andrews & McMeel, 1991.
Hughes, Shirley. *Rhymes for Annie Rose.* New York: Lothrop, Lee & Shepard, 1995.
Hughes, Shirley. *The Shirley Hughes Nursery Collection.* New York: Lothrop, Lee & Shepard, 1994.
Johnson, Crockett. *Harold and the Purple Crayon.* New York: HarperCollins, 1981.

Keats, Ezra Jack. *Dreams.* New York: Simon & Schuster, 1992.

Lester, Allison. *Imagine.* Boston: Houghton Mifflin, 1990.

McGuinness, Doreen (illustrator). *Nursery Rhymes.* Bethlehem, PA: Brimax Books, 1996.

Moore, Dessie. *Let's Pretend.* New York: HarperCollins, 1994.

Pandell, Karen. *Animal Action ABC: A Rhyme 'n' Mime Book.* New York: Dutton, 1996.

Parish, Peggy. A*melia Bedelia.* New York: HarperCollins, 1992.

Sendak, Maurice. *In the Night Kitchen.* New York: HarperCollins, 1995.

Sendak, Maurice. *Where the Wild Things Are.* New York: HarperCollins, 1988.

Seuss, Dr. *Hop on Pop.* New York: Random House, 1966.

Sweet, Melissa. *Fiddle-I-Fee: A Farmyard Song for the Very Young.* Boston: Little Brown, 1994.

MULTICULTURAL

Belpré, Pura. *Perez and Martina.* New York: Warner, 1961. (Also available in Spanish as *Perez y Martina.*)

Burton, Marilee. *My Best Shoes.* New York: Morrow, 1994.

Cummings, Pat. *My Aunt Came Back.* New York: HarperCollins, 1998.

Evans, Lezlie. *Can You Count Ten Toes? Count to 10 in 10 Different Languages.* Boston: Houghton Mifflin, 1998.

Falwell, Cathryn. *Feast for Ten.* Boston: Houghton Mifflin, 1993.

Flack, Marjorie. *The Story About Ping.* New York: Viking, 1933.

Greenfield, Eloise. *First Pink Light.* New York: Writers & Readers, 1991.

Griego, Margot C., et al. *Tortillitas Para Mama and Other Nursery Rhymes: Spanish and English.* New York: Holt, Rinehart & Winston, 1981.

Hong, Lily Toy. *Two of Everything: A Chinese Folktale.* Morton Grove, IL: Whitman, 1993.

Hudson, Cheryl W., and Bernette G. Ford. *Bright Eyes, Brown Skin.* Littleton, MA: Sundance, 1993.

Louie, Ai-Ling. *Yeh-Shen: A Cinderella Story From China.* New York: Putnam, 1990.

Mattox, Cheryl (Ed.). *Shake It to the One That You Love the Best.* Oakley, CA: Warren-Mattox, 1990.

Onyefulu, Ifeoma. *A Is for Africa.* New York: Dutton, 1993.

Oppenheim, Shulamith Levy. *Fireflies for Nathan.* New York: Morrow, 1991.

Patrick, Denise L. *Red Dancing Shoes.* New York: Morrow, 1993.

Scott, Ann H. *Sam.* New York: Putnam, 1996.

Shaik, Fatima. *On Mardi Gras Day.* New York: Dial, 1999.

OCCUPATIONS

Ahlberg, Allan and Janet. *Mrs. Wobble the Waitress.* New York: Golden Books, 1982.

Brown, Craig. *The Pathwork Farmer.* New York: Greenwillow, 1989.

Brown, Craig. *Tractor.* New York: Greenwillow, 1995.

Catalanotto, Peter. *The Painter.* New York: Orchard, 1995.

Flanagan, Alice K. *Here Comes Mr. Eventoff With The Mail!* New York: Children's Press, 1998.

Gibbons, Gail. *Say Woof.* New York: Macmillan, 1992.

Lisowski, Gabriel. *How Tevye Became a Milkman.* New York: Holt, 1976.

MacKinnon, Debbie. *What Am I?* New York: Dial, 1996.

Pellegrino, Marjorie. *My Grandma's the Mayor.* Washington, DC: Magination Press, 2000.

Rice, Eve. *Sam Who Never Forgets.* New York: Morrow, 1987.

Roop, Peter and Connie. *Stick Out Your Tongue!* Minneapolis: Lerner, 1986.

Zimmerman, Andrea, and David Clemesha. *Trashy Town.* New York: HarperCollins, 1999.

SEASONS AND DAYS OF THE WEEK

Carle, Eric. *Today Is Monday.* New York: Putnam, 1997.

Carle, Eric. *The Very Hungry Caterpillar.* New York: Putnam, 1994.

Chapman, Cheryl. S*now on Snow on Snow.* New York: Dial, 1994.

Crews, Nina. *One Hot Summer Day.* New York: Greenwillow, 1995.

Evans, Lezlie. *Rain Song.* Boston: Houghton Mifflin, 1995.

Gibbons, Gail. *The Reasons for Seasons.* New York: Holiday House, 1995.

Joosse, Barbara M. *Snow Day!* New York: Clarion Books, 1995.

Keats, Ezra Jack. *The Snowy Day.* New York: Viking, 1996.

London, Jonathan. *Froggy Gets Dressed.* New York: Viking, 1992.

McCully, Emily. *First Snow.* New York: HarperCollins, 1985.

Rockwell, Anne. *First Comes Spring.* New York: HarperCollins, 1985.

Sendak, Maurice. *Chicken Soup With Rice: A Book of Months.* New York: HarperCollins, 1991.

Shields, Carol Diggory. *Day by Day a Week Goes Round.* New York: Dutton, 1998.

Sipiera, Paul and Diane. *The Seasons.* New York: Children's Press, 1998.

Ward, Cindy. *Cookie's Week.* New York: Putnam, 1988.

Ziefert, Harriet, and Susan Baum. *I Love Summer.* New York: HarperCollins, 1992.

SHAPES, NUMBERS, COLORS, AND SPACE

Aker, Suzanne. *What Comes in 2's, 3's, and 4's?* New York: Simon & Schuster, 1992.

Anno, Mitsumasa. *Anno's Counting Book.* New York: Scholastic, 1998.

Bang, Molly. *Ten, Nine, Eight.* New York: Morrow, 1991.

Carle, Eric. *1, 2, 3 to the Zoo.* New York: Putnam, 1990.

Crews, Donald. *Ten Black Dots.* New York: Greenwillow Books, 1986.

Dodds, Dayle Ann. *The Shape of Things.* Cambridge, MA: Candlewick Press, 1996.

Feelings, Muriel. *Moja Means One: Swahili Counting Book.* New York: Dial, 1976.

Garne, S.T. *One White Sail.* New York: Simon & Schuster, 1992.

Giganti, Paul, Jr. *How Many Snails?* New York: Morrow, 1994.

Hoban, Tana. *Circles, Triangles, and Squares.* New York: Simon & Schuster, 1974.

Hoban, Tana. *Of Color and Things.* New York: Greenwillow, 1989.

Hoban, Tana. *Over, Under, and Through, and Other Spatial Concepts.* New York: Simon & Schuster, 1973.

Kitchen, Bert. *Animal Numbers.* New York: Puffin, 1991.

O'Neil, Mary. *Hailstones and Halibut Bones: Adventures in Color.* New York: Doubleday, 1961.

Van Fleet, Matthew. *One Yellow Lion.* New York: Dial, 1992.

Wilson, April. *April Wilson's Magpie Magic: A Tale of Colorful Mischief.* New York: Dial, 1999.

Anno, Mitsumasa. *Anno's Journey.* New York: Putnam, 1997.
Barton, Byron. *Airport.* New York: HarperCollins, 1982.
Bemelmans, Ludwig. *Madeline.* New York: Viking, 1993.
Carle, Eric. *Rooster's Off to See the World.* New York: Simon & Schuster, 1992.
Crews, Donald. *School Bus.* New York: Greenwillow, 1984.
Crews, Donald. *Truck.* New York: Greenwillow, 1980.
Hindley, Judy. *The Big Red Bus.* Cambridge, MA: Candlewick Press, 1995.
Jenkins, Steve. *Looking Down.* Boston: Houghton Mifflin, 1995.
Jonas, Ann. *Round Trip.* New York: Greenwillow, 1983.
Knorr, Rosanne. *If I Lived in France* (and sequels). Marietta, GA: Longstreet Press, 1994.
Lenski, Lois. *Move Mr. Small.* New York: H.Z. Walck, 1979.
McNaughton, Colin. *Walk Rabbit Walk.* New York: Morrow, 1992.
Pallotta, Jerry, and Fred Stillwell. *The Airplane Alphabet Book.* Watertown, MA: Charlesbridge, 1997.
Parish, Peggy. *Amelia Bedelia Goes Camping.* New York: Avon, 1997.
Scarry, Richard. *Richard Scarry's Cars and Trucks from A to Z.* New York: Random House, 1990.
Siebert, Diane. *Train Song.* New York: HarperCollins, 1990.

Music Recordings

Bartels, Joanie. *Dancin' Magic.* Discovery Music (Children's), 1991.
Bernstein, Leonard. *Peter and the Wolf.* Life, Times, & Music.
Blues Clues. *Blue's Big Treasure: A Musical Adventure.* Kid Rhino, 1999.
Boston Pops. *Wish Upon a Star: All-Time Children's Favorites.* Philips, 1996.
Everybody Dance! (various artists). Rhino Records, 1998.
Good Housekeeping Kids. *Classic Kids Party Songs.* Kid-Tel, 1998.
Good Housekeeping Kids. *Family Album: Musical Portraits of a Family.* Kid-Tel, 1998.
Good Housekeeping Kids. *Melody Magic for Kids.* Kid-Tel, 1998.
Good Housekeeping Kids. *Travelin' Tunes for Kids.* Kid-Tel, 1998.
Guthrie, Woody. *Songs to Grow On.* Rounder Records, 1951.
Henson, Jim. *Sesame Street Collection.* Golden Music.
Holzman, Keith (producer). *Authentic Sound Effects.* Elektra Entertainment.
Ives, Burl. *Little White Duck and Other Children's Favorites.* Sony/Columbia, 1997.
Jenkins, Ella. *Jambo and Other Call and Response Songs and Chants.* Smithsonian Folkways, 1974.
Jenkins, Ella. *You'll Sing a Song and I'll Sing a Song.* Smithsonian Folkways.
Kangaroo Kids. *Kool Songs.* Music for Little People, 1996.
Kangaroo Kids. *Krazy Songs.* Music for Little People, 1996.
Kid Songs. *A Day at Old MacDonald's Farm.* Sony/Wonder, 1997.
Kid Songs. *I Can Dance!* Sony/Wonder, 1998.
Kids' Classics. *Silly Songs.* Benson Records, 1994.
Little People Sing-Along. *Home Sweet Home.* Kid Rhino, 1997.

Parachute Express. *Happy to Be Here.* Buena Vista, 1991.

Pipillion. *Cajun for Kids.* Kid Rhino, 1998.

Positively Reggae: An All-Family Musical Celebration. Sony/Wonder, 1995.

Raffi. *More Singable Songs for the Very Young.* Rounder Records, 1977.

Raffi. *Raffi in Concert With the Rise and Shine Band.* Rounder Records, 1989.

Raffi. *Raffi on Broadway — a Family Concert.* MCA, 1993.

Raffi. *The Singable Songs for the Very Young.* Rounder Records, 1977.

Rashad, Phylicia. *Baby's Nursery Rhymes.* Lightyear, 1991.

Seeger, Mike and Peggy. *American Folk Songs for Children.* Rounder Records.

Seeger, Pete. *Abiyoyo.* Smithsonian Folkways.

Sooz. *Favorite First Songs.* Soozaroo Music, 1995.

Taj Mahal, Linda Tillery, and Eric Bibb. *Shakin' a Tailfeather.* Kid Rhino, 1997.

Thomas, Marlo, & Friends. *Free to Be... You and Me.* Arista, 1972.

Bibliography

References

Ackerman, D. (1999). *Deep play.* New York: Random House.

Dansky, J.L., & Silverman, I.W. (1973). Effects of play on associative fluency in preschool-age children. *Developmental Psychology*, Vol. 9, pp. 38-43.

Dattner, R. (1969). *Design for play.* New York: Van Nostrand Reinhold.

DeMille, R. (1973). *Put your mother on the ceiling: Children's imagination games.* New York: Viking.

Elkind, D. (1981). *The hurried child.* Boston: Addison-Wesley.

Erikson, E. (1963). *Childhood and society.* New York: Norton.

Esdaile, S.A. (1996). A play-focused intervention involving mothers of preschoolers. *American Journal of Occupational Therapy,* Vol. 50, No. 2, pp. 113-122.

Esdaile, S.A., & Sanderson, A. (1987). *Toys to make.* Ringwood, Victoria, Australia: Penguin Australia.

Freyberg, J. (1973). Increasing the imaginative play of urban disadvantaged kindergarten children through systematic training. In J.L. Singer, *The child's world of make-believe.* New York: Academic Press.

Gardner, H. (1983). *Frames of mind.* New York: Basic Books.

Garney, C. (1990). *Play.* Cambridge, MA: Harvard University Press.

Goldstein, K. (1939). *The organism.* New York: American Book Company.

Groos, K. (1976). *The play of man.* New York: Arno Press.

Guilford, J.P. (1968). *Intelligence, creativity and their educational implications.* New York: Robert K. Knapp.

Huesman, L.R. (Ed.). (1994). *Aggressive behavior: Current perspectives.* New York: Plenum Press.

Katz, S.A., & Thomas, J.A. (1996). *Teaching creativity by working the word: Language, music and movement.* Boston: Allyn & Bacon.

Lieberman, J. N. (1977). *Playfulness: Its relationship to imagination and creativity.* New York: Academic Press.

Pellegrini, A.D. (Ed.). (1995). *The future of play theory*. Albany: State University of New York Press.

Piaget, J. (1932). *The language and thought of the child*. New York: Harcourt Brace.

Piaget, J. (1962). *Play, dreams and imitation in childhood*. New York: Norton.

Rogers, F. (1994). *You are special*. New York: Viking.

Rogers, F., & Head, B. (1983). *Mr. Rogers talks with parents*. New York: Berkeley Books.

Schwartz, L.L., & Matzkin. (1999). Tuning in to the media: Youth, vioence, and incivility. In L.L. Schwartz, *Psychology and the media*. Washington DC: American Psychological Association.

Shmukler, D. (1982-83). Preschool imaginative play predisposition and its relationship to subsequent third grade assessment. *Imagination, Cognition and Personality*, Vol. 2, No. 3, pp. 231-240.

Singer, D.G. (1993). *Playing for their lives: Helping troubled children through play therapy*. New York: Free Press.

Singer, D.G., & Revenson, T.A. (1996). *A Piaget primer: How a child thinks*. New York: Plume/Penguin.

Singer, D.G., & Singer J.L. (Eds.). (2000). *Handbook of children and the media*. Thousand Oaks, CA: Sage Publications.

Singer, D.G., & Singer, J.L. (1990). *The house of make believe: Children's play and the developing imagination*. Cambridge, MA: Harvard University Press.

Singer, D.G., Singer, J.L., & Zuckerman, D. (1995). *A parent's guide: Use TV to your child's advantage*. Sarasota, FL: Acropolis South.

Singer, J.L. (1973). *The child's world of make-believe: Experimental studies of imaginative play*. New York: Academic Press.

Singer, J.L., & Singer, D.G. (1981). *Television, imagination and aggression: A study of preschoolers*. Hillsdale, NJ: Lawrence Erlbaum.

Smilansky, S. (1968). *The effects of sociodramatic play on disadvantaged preschool children*. New York: Wiley.

Sparling, J., & Lewis, I. (Eds.). (1984). *Learning games for threes and fours: A guide to adult and child play*. New York: Walker.

Sutton-Smith, B. (1972). *The folkgames of children*. Austin: University of Texas Press.

Resources

American Toy Institute. (1998). *Fun play, safe play* (guidebook). American Toy Institute, Inc., 1115 Broadway, Suite 400, New York, NY 10010.

Center for Media Education and the Henry J. Kaiser Family Foundation. (1999). *A parent's guide to the TV ratings and V-chip*. The Center for Media Education, 2120 L St., N.W., Washington, DC 20037-1527.

Council of Better Business Bureaus, Children's Advertising Review Unit. (1998). *Self-regulatory guidelines for children's advertising*. Council of Better Business Bureaus, Inc., 845 Third Ave., New York, NY 10022.

ERIC Clearinghouse on Disabilities and Gifted Education, 1920 Association Dr., Reston, VA 22091 (1-800-328-0272).

Hill, P. *Creative playground*. Children's Environment Advisory Service, Central Mortgage and Housing Corporation Head Office, Ottawa, Ontario K1A 0P7, Canada.

National Association for the Education of Young Children, 1509 16th St., NW, Washington, DC 20036 (1-800-424-2460).

National Information Center for Children and Youth with Disabilities, P.O. Box 1492, Washington, DC 20013-1492 (1-800-695-0285, voice and TTY).

U.S. Department of Education (1997). *Parents' guide to the internet* (publication no. MIS97-6609). Washington, DC: Office of Educational Research and Improvement, U.S. Department of Education.

U.S. Department of Education Resource Center, 1-800-USA LEARN, or 1-877-4-ED-PUBS. (Good source for books and manuals pertaining to the education of children.)

Credits

Editor: Darcie Conner Johnston. Art Director: Susan K. White. Text editing assistance was provided by Paul Chance, Ph.D., and Margaret Schlegel. The sources for the photographs, illustrations, and images are as follows: Front cover, pages 6-10, 21, 25: © 1999 Eyewire, Inc. Page 26: art by Fred Holz. Pages 31, 35: © 1999 Eyewire, Inc. Page 38: art by Linda Bronson, © 1999 Artville, LLC. Page 41: art by Fred Holz. Page 49: © 1999 Eyewire, Inc. Pages 51, 52, 54: image by Susan K. White. Pages 56, 57: art by Fred Holz. Page 58: image courtesy Lena J. Figlear. Page 59: art by Fred Holz. Page 60: art by Linda Bronson, © 1999 Artville, LLC. Page 63: © 1999 Eyewire, Inc. Page 66: image by Susan K. White. Page 67: art by Linda Bronson, © 1999 Artville, LLC. Page 70: image by Susan K. White. Page 71: art by Fred Holz. Pages 74-75: image by Susan K. White. Page 77: © Eyewire, Inc. Page 79: art by Fred Holz. Page 81: © 1999 Eyewire, Inc. Pages 82, 83: art by Fred Holz. Pages 84, 85: art by Linda Bronson, © 1999 Artville, LLC. Pages 86-87: art by Fred Holz. Page 89: © 1999 Eyewire, Inc. Pages 92, 94, 96, 97: art by Fred Holz. Page 99: © 1999 Eyewire, Inc. Page 103: image by Susan K. White. Pages 104, 105, 107: art by Fred Holz. Page 108: images by Susan K. White. Page 109: art by Fred Holz. Page 111: art by Linda Bronson, © 1999 Artville, LLC. Page 112: image by Susan K. White. Page 115: art by Fred Holz. Pages 117, 119: © 1999 Eyewire, Inc. Page 121: art by Linda Bronson, © 1999 Artville, LLC. Page 122: photo by Susan K. White. Page 124: art by Fred Holz; image by Susan K. White. Page 127: art by Fred Holz. Pages 128, 131: image by Susan K. White. Pages 132, 133: art by Fred Holz. Pages 135, 136, 139: © 1999 Eyewire, Inc. Page 141: image by Susan K. White. Pages 142, 143, 145, 147: image by Susan K. White. Page 148: art by Fred Holz. Pages 149, 150-151: image by Susan K. White. Page 153: © 1999 Eyewire, Inc. Page 157: Photograph of "Ernie," *Sesame Street*, © 2000 Sesame Workshop. Sesame Street Muppets, © 2000 Jim Henson Company. Page 158: Photograph of Fred Rogers, *Mister Rogers' Neighborhood*, courtesy of Family Communications, Inc. Photo by Walt Seng. Page 161: Photograph of *Barney & Friends*, © 1997 Lyons Partnership, L.P. All rights reserved. Pages 163, 167: art by Fred Holz.

ACKNOWLEDGMENTS

We wish to acknowledge the assistance of Lisa Pagliaro and Sharon Plaskon for their diligent word processing of the manuscript. We thank Patrice Farquharson and Carmen Rodriguez, early childhood specialists, for their careful reading of the text and comments and suggestions. We are also indebted to dozens of preschool teachers who employed these games and exercises as part of our various research projects with hundreds of children in New Haven, Connecticut, and in cities across the United States.